£10·95

New Futures

Mary Hughes has worked in further and community education, and has been active in the Women's Liberation Movement for over 10 years. She is currently working for the Inner London Adult Education Service as a head of centre.

Mary Kennedy has taught and worked in a variety of educational institutions in the last 20 years as well as being involved in local community activities. She has been a feminist since 1970. She is now women's studies tutor in the Extra-Mural Department of London University.

Case studies from: Dorothy Eagleson, Juliet McCaffery, Saroj Seth, Sally Griffiths, Hilary Tinley and Sue Walker, Gill Boden, Sue Owen, Beverley Evans, Rita Cordon and Liz Cousins, Madeleine Dickens, Anne Chiew Yean Khoo, Pauline Imrie, Diana Derioz, Joy Rose, Ally Jones, Liverpool Women's Education Centre, The South-West London Women's Studies Group, Pat Bould and Clare Manifold, Diana Leonard.

MOVEMENT

Towards not being
anyone else's center
of gravity.
            A wanting
to love: not
to lean over towards
an other, and fall,
but feel within one
a flexible steel
upright, parallel
to the spine but
longer, from which to stretch;
one's own
grave springboard; the outflying spirit's
vertical trampoline

                        Denise Levertov

New Futures

Changing Women's Education

Mary Hughes and Mary Kennedy

Routledge & Kegan Paul

London, Boston, Melbourne and Henley

This book is for women who work and learn together

Also from Mary H. – to Isabel for yesterday;
Jane for today;
Annie Rose for tomorrow

First published in 1985
by Routledge & Kegan Paul plc

14 Leicester Square, London WC2H 7PH, England

9 Park Street, Boston, Mass. 02108, USA

464 St Kilda Road, Melbourne,
Victoria 3004, Australia and

Broadway House, Newtown Road,
Henley on Thames, Oxon RG9 1EN, England

Set in Baskerville
by Columns of Reading
and printed in Great Britain

Library of Congress Cataloging in Publication Data

New futures.
Bibliography: p.
Includes index.
1. Adult education of women – Great Britain – Ad-
dresses, essays, lectures. 2. Women's studies – Great
Britain – Addresses, essays, lectures. I. Hughes, Mary,
1951-   . II. Kennedy, Mary, 1931-
LC1666.G7N48   1985   376'.941   84-22347

British Library CIP data also available

ISBN 0-7102-0612-7 (c)
ISBN 0-7100-9988-6 (Pbk)

Contents

Acknowledgments xi

Poem: 'Movement' xii

Introduction 1

Part I 7

1 Lifecycles: A Positive Model of Fragmentation 9
2 Women's Education – Women's Studies 24
3 Where Women are, and Where are Women in Adult Education? 43

Part II Case Studies 55

Section 1 Access 57

 1 The Educational Guidance Service for Adults in Northern Ireland *Dorothy Eagleson: additions by the authors* 57
 2 Women in Literacy and Adult Basic Education: Barriers to Access *Juliet McCaffery* 62
 3 Education of Asian Women *Saroj Seth* 69

Section 2 Courses 75

 4 Breakaway: A Discussion Group for Women *Sally Griffiths* 75

5 Sandwich Course for Part-time Tutors of Dress
or Embroidery at Loughborough College of Art
and Design   *Hilary Tinley and Sue Walker*   78

6 Women in Public Life – Leadership Training
Gill Boden   82

Section 3   Extending the Subject   86

7 Working with Childminders   *Sue Owen*   86

8 The Sheffield Clothing Co-operative – PREMTOGS
Beverley Evans   90

9 Women and New Technology – Where are we
going? – A New Course for Women in Liverpool
Rita Cordon and Liz Cousins   92

10 Women and Skill Centres – The Deptford
Experience   *Madeleine Dickens*   95

Section 4   Women in Centres   99

11 Chinese Women on Merseyside
Anne Chiew Yean Khoo   99

12 The Women's Education Centre, Southampton
*Pauline Imrie, on behalf of the Women's Education
Collective*   102

13 The Totnes Women's Centre – A Personal
Experience   *Diana Derioz*   104

Section 5   Processes   110

14 Women and Education Group, Manchester
*Joy Rose, on behalf of the Women's Education
Collective*   110

15 The Workers Educational Association (WEA) and
Women's Education   *Ally Jones*   113

16 Liverpool Women's Education Centre
By Themselves   118

17 The South-West London Women's Studies
Group   *By Themselves*   126

18 New Opportunities for Women – Setting up a
Course – A Personal View
Pat Bould and Clare Manifold   130

19 'The Changing Experience of Women' at the
Open University   *Diana Leonard*   135

Contents

vii

Part III 143

4   What sort of Education? What Sort of Culture?   145

5   Dilemmas of Innovation   160

Appendix: Safe and Sound   172

Bibliography   176

Index   182

Acknowledgments

We owe thanks for help, support and ideas to so many that we hope they will feel included within the dedication. But we are especially grateful to the following:

to the Case Study writers who trusted us and helped make this book better;

to past and present students for teaching us so much;

to women working in adult education, especially in the ILEA, in the Extra-Mural Department, London University, and the WEA who have shared ideas and struggles, given advice and extended our horizons by their example;

to those who gave of their time, and allowed us to try out ideas in interviews: Caroline Bailey, Joanna Bornat, some students from Hillcroft College in the summer of 1983, Enid Hutchinson, Phoebe Lambert, Margaret Marshall, Barbara Saunders and Jack Taylor;

to Pippa Brewster, John Ford, Renate Duelli Klein, Bill Kennedy, Ruth Lesirge and Dale Spender who read the drafts, and offered constructive criticisms and encouragement;

to Mary Cooper, Rita Hann and Sue Castagnetti who patiently typed and re-typed our messy manuscripts: without them we could not have survived into print;

for specific help in finding books and material we thank Beverley Campbell, Howard Fisher, Elizabeth Gerver, Elaine Pole, Rose Taw and Jane Thompson;

and finally to our families and friends for their support, patient endurance, and for keeping the coffee pot replenished.

Any mistakes and omissions are ours.

We are grateful for permission to print the following extracts: To Denise Levertov for her poem, 'Movement', from her book, *Life in the Forest*, copyright © 1978 by Denise Levertov, reprinted by permission of New Directions Publishing Corp. And to *SIGNS: Journal of Women in Culture and Society, University of Chicago*.

Introduction

This is a book above movement, about breaking the silence of women in education. It raises issues about where women are, where they might be, and how education as a process can be used for women. We focus on women and have not given specific space to men, because books about education for adults are generally written for and about men; women appear as a special sub-species in the index. Yet women are there and in the majority, unlike the situation in further and higher education. It is often easier to argue the case that women are discriminated against when they are absent – in parts of the work force, for example, or not differentiated from men in the statistics. But in adult education women are present, therefore we have the problem of convincing men and women that there is discrimination and that the kinds of education women have is not necessarily right or appropriate: neither in the present nor for the future. But change is possible and is essential. We cannot know exactly what the end product might look like if women determined their own education. But we predict that being involved in the process, planning and deciding upon their own learning would make women aware of the limited choices open to them at present. We suspect they would insist on doing things differently.

Wherever women are or come from they all lead fragmented lives because of the multiplicity of roles they have and the expectations put upon them. This fragmentation is potentially a positive characteristic, which, if it were transferred into men's lives as well and acknowledged as important and valid, could result in a reshaping of attitudes about life and work patterns. It would also relate more appropriately to a time where full-time employment will probably never again be a reality, and relationships between women and men will, of necessity, have to change. We have tried to point to some of the dilemmas involved in creative change by suggesting a radical re-appraisal of the education of women, which must have repercussions for the education of men and children as well.

There is a difficulty about defining what is women's education. It has always been decided for them by others, according to the prevailing stereotypic expectations of society, of who women are and what their roles should be. They have to fit into acceptable moulds according to their class, their age and their servicing role in the family. Biology gets in the way. In many senses Rousseau's prescription still subtly influences education today:

> A woman's education must therefore be planned in relation to man. To be pleasing in his sight, to win his respect and love, to train him in childhood, to tend him in manhood, to counsel and console him, to make his life pleasant and happy, *these are the duties of woman for all time*, and this is what she should be taught while she is young. The further we depart from this principle, the further we shall be from our goal, and *all our precepts will fail to secure her happiness or our own.* (Rousseau: 1982:328) (our italics)

This is an example, we think, of the dominant (male) ideology providing its own interpretation of the purposes of education, which neglects women's views and needs.

Today the debates over education for women differ in content from those of earlier centuries. These were originally concerned with whether women were educable (did they have minds even?). What kind of education was suitable for them and to what end, and at what level (compare early nineteenth-century attitudes on the education of the working classes)? If they were to be admitted to higher education would this over-tax their brains and bodies, unwoman them? Or, at the other end of the class scale, would general education lead them to neglect their female duties in life? So both schools and evening institutes in the latter half of the nineteenth century provided domestic education within the 'separate sphere' tradition. This is where the case more or less rested until the advent of the modern women's liberation movement in the late 1960s. Currently it is, at least in theory, conceded that girls and women have the right to equal access to all kinds of study and subjects, although the expectations and practices are such that this will not radically alter the existing educational provision. And indeed in adult education women still continue to take up the arts, languages, humanities and social studies, particularly in university adult education, alongside a minority of men. They are also the majority in the domestic and recreational subjects provided by the local education authorities (LEAs). But now feminists in education have begun 'The task of creating knowledge in which the experiences of men stopped being the measure and called the one of "people". Women were to be seen as "people" too, and it was women's questions that were being asked' (Duelli-Klein: 1984).

Feminists thus joined the radical education debate questioning the double standards of education and challenging its claims to neutrality and balance and its hidden class, race and sex bias. They have begun the process of uncovering the conscious/ unconscious and internalised male centredness of our society. By doing this feminists are challenging the misogynous bias and illogicalities embedded in education and other institutions.

Our proposition is that all education must recognise the full contribution of women, not only as object but as subject too: that men should be studied differently; that there is no such thing as sex-blind subject disciplines; or that the education process is neutral.

It is true that there is some confusion about the term women's education. This has been used to describe traditional female education centring around the home, and physical, art and recreation subjects. This limiting definition obscures the issue since women's education must be much broader, drawing upon many disciplines, than merely educating women to continue as they always have. We identify four strands in women's education: extending traditional subjects both male and female; education that is positive discrimination; women's studies/feminist studies classes for women about women and by women; and a feminist dimension in all education and its practices. It is not just a question of simple equality or more access to more of the same education, but a qualitative change of emphasis where the many dimensions of women's experiences and knowledge, alongside those of other races and cultures, are taken as natural, normal, and universal.

In education this difficult process has been generated by women's studies. These are an integral part of women's education and of education generally, but they have a different purpose and mode of being within it. Women's studies are difficult to define because there are as many different definitions as there are of education. Our own working definition is that women's studies/ feminist studies are the study of power and gender relationships between women and men, past and present, and that they take a contextual approach, meaning that both the content and the process of learning together as women are equally important.

New kinds and forms of education are essential if people are to adapt to and have some influence in the post-industrial society that technology will force upon us. For the last two hundred years education has been linked to the needs of an industrial, work-directed and individualist consumer society where technical and economic needs were paramount. Today we think that the new frontiers for education are in the social and psychological areas, and concern for the quality of life. The recurring argument is that women's experiences and knowledge are a liberating example for a new kind of society and new flexible forms of education.

This book takes up the ideas and experiences of women in order to involve the reader, as well as the adult educator, in fresh ways of educational thinking, seeing and doing. We have tried to get away from the commonly held assumptions that where women are seen and discussed they are analysed en masse rather than as individuals or groups coming from varied cultures and religions, generations and lifestyles, and economic backgrounds as do men.

We would have liked to have followed the lessons learned from the women's liberation movement more closely in the process of making this book – taking a collective and co-operative approach in writing it. But this was not possible because we wished to include examples of women's educational initiatives and practices from all over the United Kingdom. Distances, time (we both have full-time jobs) and money made this impracticable. So we have opened up the central section of the book to enable women both individually and collectively to write in their own voices about their educational experiences, and because what they say is important and useful. We have tried but were unsuccessful in finding a case study where black women wrote about their experiences of learning together as black women. Little space has been given to the concerns and issues of minority women – not because we were unaware of this omission but we lacked the knowledge and experience to do this ourselves. Also we felt strongly that minority women would want to state their case in their own ways. It would have been racist of us and only a token gesture if we had discussed their issues from the outside in a cursory manner.

For ourselves the struggles, the exhilarations, the despairs and the delays, combined with the fragmented lives we both lead, have been a learning experience. The sharing of knowledge and new ideas in a non-competitive manner symbolises for us how the women's liberation movement has influenced the ways in which women study and write together.

We have tried to move the arguments and evidence for women's education forward, relying greatly on the ideas and work already done by other women. In a way we have posed more questions than we have answers for at present, but we hope that by suggesting new approaches, floating embryonic ideas, others will take these up and develop them more fully.

Part I

Chapter 1
Lifecycles: A Positive Model of Fragmentation

It is one of the ironies and injustices of life that women are 'probably the most discussed animal in the Universe' (Woolf (1929): 1983: 27). They are catalogued, indexed, researched, described, prescribed for, circumscribed by, criticised and defined by philosophers, psychologists, reformers, clerics, authors, judges, researchers, teachers and the 'ordinary men' who set themselves up as experts on the subject of women.

WOMEN

Woman is a Riddle / A Woman is a Weathercock

The Woman Movement / A Woman named Louise
    / A Woman Named Solitude

A Woman of Fifty
A Woman of Genius
A Woman of Letters
A Woman of Means

The Woman of my Life / A Woman of no Importance
A Woman of Parts; memories
of a life on stage

Woman of Property
Woman of Spirit
Woman of Straw
A Woman of Taste

The Woman of the Twilight
The Woman of Valor
Woman of Violence
Woman on her Own

Woman Turned Bully

A Woman Unashamed

Woman Under Monasticism
Woman Under Socialism

The Woman Voter
The Woman Wage Earner
Woman with a Future

The Woman Who Could not Read
The Woman Who Did
The Woman Who Lost Him
The Woman Who Rode Away

The Woman Who Spends
The Woman Who Waits

        The Woman Who Toils

Woman With a Future

      The Woman With the Whip
      The Woman Within
      The Woman You Want to be

Womanpower is one word

(This is taken from a recent longer poem by an American poet – Loreen McGrail. She found it more or less in alphabetical order in the University of Oregon Library.)

It seems obvious, but we do ask why men as a separate species are not picked out as a suitable subject for treatment or study? The answer is that men define and make the world in their own image, so women, like black people, children and other named groups, are a sub-species deviating from the norm – normal which is male. For, as Susan Lipshitz has pointed out, the images of women and men in our society result in making women seem deficient.

> For stereotypic femininity describes women as more passive, weak, expressive of emotion, dependent, illogical and living in a world of feeling and far more concerned with their own appearance than are men. The male stereotype emphasises competence, activity, analytic ability and independence – all characteristics that are considered to be both socially desirable and adult. (Lipshitz: 1978: 96)

Not enough attention is paid to the ways in which women see themselves. Naturally there is an enormous diversity of views and experience since women are half the human race and therefore as different among themselves as are men. The tendency has been to view them as one group or an amorphous whole. In addition they are generally perceived and constructed into a limited strait-jacket of roles: the stereotypes of mother, wife, sister, daughter, mistress, whore, virgin and spinster. Women are rarely described by the work they do. The first four categories here are so often used to describe women in the possessed dependent sense as some-body's. . . . The remaining four categories have a derogatory sexual implication. As Julia Stanley (quoted in Spender: 1980: 15) found, there were 'two hundred and twenty words (in the English language) for a sexually promiscuous female and only twenty for a sexually promiscuous male'. There are other alternative words which have a more positive and less sexist connotation: lover instead of mistress; prostitute seems less emotive and more professional than whore; celibate rather than spinster implies choice rather than deficiency. And the state of virginity is surely a man-made conception, rather than taking the ancient meaning of the word which is 'she-who-is-unto-herself'? (Rich: 1977: 249). This description, seemingly so simple and direct, points up all kinds of complex questions about how women see themselves, find an identity, within the maze of ways in which they are defined and confined. It is not our purpose (nor is it within our knowledge) to examine in any depth how psychologists have researched this area of being, since we are concentrating upon women and the role that education does and could play in making sense of the confusion and doubts in their lives. But before change can take place the problems must be understood. There is a lack of research at present on the psychological attitudes and identity of the mature woman student[1] in adult, as distinct from higher education.[2] Indeed there has not been much in-depth research on adult education generally, compared with other sections of education. This is probably because of the predominance of the child-centred psychologists in education, as well as adult education's real or assumed marginality within the education service.[3]

In the wider field feminist psychologists[4] have now begun to analyse critically the hypotheses, research, methodology and findings on 'female psychology' and identity. All of this new work, which has cross-cultural and sociological implications as well, examines rigorously the invisible as well as the visible male bias in research, and constructively proposes new ways of seeing, questioning and interpreting sex role stereotyping, behavioural patterns, social conditioning and role relationships. Women need to be liberated from always being measured against men and therefore always being found deficient. They need to find their own yardstick and their own psychological space and identity.

The question of values

We should be aware of what is described as women's lack of confidence, their lack of conscious selfhood which makes them appear less assertive than men in mixed groupings. There are many situations, committees especially, where the few women present will contribute to the discussions with the introductory 'maybe' phrases: 'This may not be relevant'. . . ; 'I may have missed the point but'. . . ; 'I may have misunderstood.' Often they are not heard; sometimes there is a pause to listen for a moment and then the discussion continues, ignoring the intervention. So women grow silent. In psychoanalytical and Marxist terms this is described as alienation. (See also Spender: 1980, and the Dutch film, *A Question of Silence*: 1983.)

Carol Gilligan suggests that 'The difficulty women experience in finding or speaking publicly *in their own voices* emerges repeatedly in the form of qualification and self-doubt, but also in intimations of a divided judgement, a *public* assessment and *private* assessment which are fundamentally at odds' (Gilligan: 1982: 16) (our italics). Some of this interpretation is based on an important study by Martina Horner in 1972 who found that young college women in the United States 'feared success' in a competitive setting which might result in loss of femininity and/or social rejection (Horner: 1972: 157-76). However, Gilligan and others argue that this feminine anxiety about achievement and success indicates a different set of values from that of the commonly accepted (male) scale: that women are aware of the 'emotional costs at which success achieved through competition is often gained' (Sassen in Gilligan: 1982: 15). This could be ascribed to a different and equally valid perception of morality. What are the human implications of a social action – rather than the question of legal justice in the absolute sense? As Virginia Woolf observed: 'It is obvious that the values of woman differ very often from the values which have been made by the other sex' (Woolf: (1929): 1983: 70). The question of different values is beautifully illustrated by Hélène Cixous's account of an old Chinese story:

> It reminds me of a little Chinese story. Every detail of this story counts. I've borrowed it from a very serious text, Sun Tse's manual of strategy, which is a kind of handbook for the warrior. This is the anecdote. The King commanded General Sun Tse: 'You who are a great strategist and claim to be able to train anybody in the arts of war . . . take my wives (all one hundred and eighty of them!) and make soldiers out of them.' We don't know why the King conceived this desire – it's the one thing we don't know . . . it remains precisely 'un(re)countable' or unaccountable in the story. But it is a King's wish, after all.
>
> So Sun Tse had the women arranged in two rows, each headed by one of the two favourite wives, and then taught them the language of the drumbeat. It was very simple: two beats – right, three beats – left, four beats – about turn or backward march. But instead of learning the code very quickly the ladies started laughing and chattering and paying no attention to the lesson, and Sun Tse, the master, repeated the lesson several times over. But the more he spoke, the more the women fell about laughing, upon which Sun Tse put his code to the test. It is said in this code that should women fall about laughing instead of becoming soldiers, their actions might be deemed mutinous, and the code has ordained that cases of mutiny call for the death penalty. So the women were condemned to death.

This bothered the King somewhat: a hundred and eighty wives are a lot to lose! He didn't want his wives to be put to death. But Sun Tse replied that since he was put in charge of making soldiers out of the women, he would carry out the order: Sun Tse was a man of absolute principle. And in any case there's an order even more 'royal' than that of the King himself: the Absolute Law. . . . One does not go back on an order. He therefore acted according to the code and with his saber beheaded the two women commanders. They were replaced and the exercise started again, and as if they had never done anything except practice the art of war, the women turned right, left, and about in silence and with never a single mistake.

It's hard to imagine a more perfect example of a particular relationship between two economies: a masculine economy and a feminine economy, in which the masculine is governed by a rule that keeps time with two beats, three beats, four beats, with pipe and drum, exactly as it should be. An order that works by inculcation, by education: it's always a question of education. An education that consists of trying to make a soldier out of the feminine by force, the force history keeps reserved for women, the 'capital' force that is effectively decapitation. Women have no choice other than to be decapitated, and in any case the moral is that if they don't actually lose their heads by the sword, *they only keep them on condition that they lose them* – lose them, that is, to complete silence, turned into automatons. (Cixous: 1981: 42-3)

These insights are important in beginning to understand the different perceptions and value systems of women, which we are still in the exploratory stage of searching out and analysing more fully. These should not be dismissed as just 'female intuition', but should rather be tackled by asking: what is missing or what elements are lacking from the moral values of the western world? Attitudes and values are still seen 'as in a glass, darkly' where women are concerned.

The value of fragmented life experiences

Women's diversity of roles and relationships are under-valued and rarely recognised as positive and creative. Their lives are seen as unimportant, lacking purpose, fulfilling only in maternity, and fragmented. But we would suggest that the reverse could be true with a change in attitude. The fragmentation in most women's lives is actually a positive and creative model for change and development, since it flexibly fits the changing lifecycles of people and the technological revolution we are living through. Within the home women are not only wives and mothers but also have an amazing number of jobs centred around the family: nurse, cook, handywoman, teacher, gardener, cleaner, chauffeur, secretary, receptionist, childminder, carer, laundress, lover, economic adviser, purchasing manager, and therapist. Additionally, apart from their immediate family, it is often forgotten that women, whether single or married, have to look after elderly dependent relatives. In a survey on North Tyneside in 1979-80 it was found that one in four of the adult women were 'carers' at that time with very little support from statutory agencies. (*New Society*: 8 September 1983: 359). Furthermore women from home negotiate with the authorities outside: insurance agents, the bank, 'the Council', the doctor, teachers, electricians, gasman, plumber, builder, and so the list goes on. They are also responsible for linking into the wider family and community networks: these include not only mediating and keeping relationships sweet within the family and maintaining contact with friends, but also possibly working with community groups, tenants' or residents' associations, political parties, voluntary women's organisations, churches and other locally based clubs and societies.

Many women with family responsibilities also work outside the home, either full time or part time: in 1982 15 per cent of mothers with dependent children worked full time and 35 per cent part time (General Household Survey 1984: 106). Yet even here, in spite of the double job burden, they still tend overwhelmingly to put home and family duties first; it is the mother who is absent from work to look after a sick child or elderly relative or to wait for the repairman to call. So they do not identify themselves primarily with their job status outside the home nor do they speak openly of the efficiency needed to combine both work roles. It is hard to be a whole person when so many demands and expectations are made upon women. But Julia Berryman quotes research that 'finds that women with a *large number of role obligations* are less likely to adopt the sick role, and in particular (C.A. Nathanson) notes that employment has the most clearly positive effects on women's health. Thus the more a woman departs from the traditional female role (housewife) a less frequent reporting of symptoms would be predicted' (Berryman: 1981: 14). Women's low esteem of themselves and their skills is because they have never fully recognised the complexities and value of their varied roles in life; neither, of course, have men.

Men are more secure in their identity, or seem to be so. Their roles in life are less complex but carry greater status. This derives from their gender identity as male: as worker/breadwinner; as husband/father/head of the household; and even their social role as perhaps an expert in local affairs, some hobby, sport or interest. Their compartmented lives allow more space, and time for them to concentrate and perfect their skills. In addition they have unquestioned privileges as males in our society and of course the support of women in all roles. But in many ways their roles are limited. For example if they are seen primarily as workers tied into a life-pattern of fifty years' paid employment, and only secondly as a husband and father, they may lose out on the fullest involvement in family relationships. Only when they are older, retired or made redundant, thus losing their status and their identification with the work they used to do, does the family become more important to them. In fact, evidence shows that the sexes grow closer together in characteristics and attitudes in old age, and something like a role reversal takes place (BBC Radio 4: *The Sexes*, Programme 6 on 'Sex and Age': 12 December 1980).

Research also shows that male friendships can be more impersonal, related more to shared interests, and therefore in many ways, not as intimate or supportive as women's networks.

As in many other studies, we found a sizeable difference between men and women. Women friends talk, drink coffee, exchange confidences and provide social support; men friends play squash, help each other, and do things together. There is less disclosure and intimacy. As well as having less intimate friendships, men also have fewer friends, especially during middle age. The reasons for these sex differences are not agreed. It could be male fear of homo-sexuality, male competitiveness at work and sport, work contacts meeting the same needs; or it may be that women have greater skills at providing it. (Argyle: in *New Society*: 21 June 1983. See also Lillian Faderman: *Surpassing the Love of Men*: 1981, for some fascinating insights into and examples of friendship between women.)

But in spite of this, men's activities and lives are considered to be more interesting, more purposeful, more fulfilling and more coherent than women's because they take place usually in the public sphere.

The adaptability of women is, in a contradictory way, both over-exploited in the home and under-used in the world outside. This flexibility to adapt creatively and supportively to circumstances is an important human resource. And the ability to be able to change directions in work, organization and relationships as needed should not be seen as a sign of weakness, but in the positive sense of acting upon and within the variety of possible alternatives in life. A recognition of this female model might mean, for instance, that there could be less friction in industrial relations, less litigation in the courts, fewer territorial wars and a diminution of bureaucracy in education.

The multiplicity of women's roles and activities could lead, if recognised, to a higher valuation being accorded to people's life experience, knowledge and the wisdom gained from this. Such a revolution would benefit the social system as well as other majority-minority groups who are seen as somehow deficient: the working class, black communities, the disabled. It would mean a more generous interpretation of people's experience which should be incorporated in assessments of what they can contribute to paid jobs, voluntary, community and creative work. And it would stop the hideous waste of abilities and human potential which now gets ignored because our sex, race, class and culture (education) define us as someone who has not conformed to the set pattern, who lack the right credentials. Such a change of values would enrich and more importantly would be *most practical* since women and men could move in and out of family, work and other roles without loss of self-respect, and without the restrictions of rigid stereotyping. This practicality would better suit the inevitable decline in jobs, the shorter-paid working hours, the slowly developing practice of serial careers and mid-life changes, serial marriages or non-contractual relationships, and the longer life expectancy of everybody in a post-industrial society.[6] There would be less alienation from the community on the part of women, youth, ethnic groups, as such new lifestyles and less hierarchical forms of power-sharing developed. This multi-dimensional life experience links in with all sorts of new possibilities for women and men and would seem to fit in more naturally with human biological cycles. As Caroline Bailey put it, 'I find I much enjoy doing numbers of different, unrelated things because I find one spins off against the other' (Interview, May, 1983).

There needs to be an alteration in people's recognition of the positive role model of the fragmentation of women's lives; and in their understanding and appreciation of the flexibility and possibilities it offers for the lives of everybody. If this does not happen then women will remain trapped in their invisible fragmentation, caught in the private world where they are waiting for others, where they have no space or time to themselves, nor outlets to make use of the positive aspects and experiences of their lives for creative, exploratory work and development. If we can break down the compartmented divisions of women's and men's lives, the 'separate spheres' ideology, then connections can be made and a more whole society created afresh. The benefit men would gain from taking on some roles women now experience would free them from the restrictions of their masculine work lives and free them from the fears of being unmanly. They have nothing to lose but the chains their fathers forged for them. For example, shared work and family responsibilities – half timing – can be enjoyable and practical. By this we do not mean role reversal but *role sharing*, for role reversal can trap both women and men in other stereotypes (see Jessie Bernard: 1972: 160-77). It is only when there is no choice, no sharing, no time off, that it becomes a duty and a chore. But attitudes and prejudices have to change.

But, it will be argued, such fragmented living will impede the attainment of the full person, the whole human being, often described by philosophers as 'homo universal'. There will be no time to get skills, be professional, become creative. We propose that, on the contrary, it is the variety of roles carried by women at present and their openness to different levels of experience in daily life which is a positive model to adopt and adapt for a fuller and richer life for all in the future.

Might There Not Have Been Other Marvels?

I spoke not only of the loss in literature, but to other fields of human knowledge and action as well, because comprehensions possible out of motherhood (including, among so much invaluable else, *the very nature, needs, illimitable potentiality of the human being – and the everyday means by which these are* distorted, discouraged, limited, extinguished) have never had the circumstances to come to powerful, undeniable, useful expression – have had instead to remain inchoate, fragmentary, unformulated (and alas invalidated). (Olsen: 1980: 202)

Lifecycles

The problem is that western society is a misogynous society that downgrades women as appendages to men with a heavy emphasis on their sexuality rather than on their human qualities and abilities (see Colvill: 1978, for a fuller discussion). Women are not only disadvantaged because of their sex, but also because of their age. As they grow older and become less sexually womanly in male-defined terms, so they are not seen to increase in experience as would be the case with men: the grey-haired man denotes wisdom, but a grey-haired woman implies ageing. A well-built man stands for health and good feeding; a well-built woman is someone who has let herself go. Susan Sontag points up the situation. 'For most women, ageing means a humiliating process of gradual sexual disqualification. Since women are considered maximally eligible in early youth, after which their sexual value drops steadily, even young women feel themselves in a desperate race against the calendar' (quoted by Hutter and Williams: 1981: 195-6). Women are divided off in terms of age and sexual status connected with each particular episode or period in the lifecycle.

Two examples out of many show the biased ways in which women can be observed or left out. No doubt Tom Lovett in his important book, *Adult Education, Community Development and the Working Class* (first published in 1975 and republished in 1982) was unaware of the way he used language to describe women, although he was not unaware of class and race. He describes the women in a Mothers' Club as 'the girls' whilst the wife of a professor was referred to as 'the lady concerned' (Lovett: 1982: 90 and 91). Further on in the same chapter in discussing education and group work he talks in neutral terms about

dealing with problems of personal morality, the role in the family, women in society, etc. It was necessary to start with people as they were and to move out. . . . It is necessary in such learning situations to think more about the student, *his* background, *his* feelings, *his* possible reactions than is usually the case in formal adult education. In the latter, it is often the tutor, *his* subject, *his* method that is important. (Lovett: 1982: 94. Lovett's italics)

The second example is in the Advisory Council for Adult and Continuing Education (ACACE) Report, *Adults: Their Educational Experiences and Needs*, published in 1982. In a comment on adult participation in post-full-time education by age and social class the Report notes: '. . . more AB women than AB men were actually in full-time education at the moment possibly because of greater availability of leisure time and a desire to "catch up" with the husband' (ACACE: 1982: 16).

The report was commenting primarily on class differences, but in the process it reveals two commonly held assumptions: that women have more leisure time than men, and that they are motivated only in relation to the men in their lives and do nothing of their own volition.

At present educational provision, both formal and informal, is based on general assumptions of what is needed by adults, or for women in the specific women's education programme. Little attention is paid, not only to the fragmented lifestyles and responsibilities of women, but also to women's lifecycles which are different from men's. The two sexes do not synchronise at the same time in the lifecycle.

Women's lifelines tend to be criss-crossed, blurred, seemingly confused, and although we have identified the multiplicity of women's roles, these are not separately valued but jumbled together in the sole role of homemaker. Men's life patterns tend to run in parallel and rarely come together: work is separated from home and home from leisure, so men's lives are divided in terms of roles and status; they have space but little connection between these different parts. They are accorded more recognition, but in reality their lives can be more limiting emotionally. In fact educational provision for adults reflects the dichotomy between work and leisure (man's experience?), rather than relating to the multi-dimensional variety of women's lives.

We would argue that, on the whole, providers of education do not appear to recognise that life is not evolutionary but is fragmented by times of reassessment and changes of direction which require different learning opportunities. This is most likely to happen in the time spans shown. Most educational planning does not make it easy for the programmes to be geared into the life patterns of women. For example it is normally assumed that girls are somehow deficient for not fitting into the accepted school examination patterns because puberty and attendant maturation occur at different times for girls and boys. But the argument could be phrased differently. That the school educational structures are made to suit boys primarily rather than girls? In the same way the structure of formal education for adults presupposes an universalist approach, which is based on the male lifecycle model, without fully appreciating the varying needs of women at different periods of their lives. It assumes that the education programmes will suit anyone, which is rather like saying that everyone can enjoy the same food. This means educators must be aware of the different lifestyle, cultural values, class and race of women students when planning their programmes.

Overleaf is a simplified model of the key points in women's lives where education may be helpful. They are not the only point of

A MODEL OF WOMEN'S EDUCATIONAL LIFECYCLES

(Starting where the student is but how much questioning of where the student is going?)

Single/Young	Young/Married/Single Parents →	Middle Aged	Young/Old	Elderly
		Displaced woman/homemaker		
		(Naturally this includes women alone)		
Few responsibilities for others	Children	Children at school/↔ return to paid work or part time work? Other interests.	Elderly dependents to care for	Dependent on others/ alone
Earnings/unemployed	Dependants?	Losing children; gaining elderly dependents	Reviving family and friendship links; retiring from paid work; voluntary work; how to adapt to the ageing process and develop psychologically	How to maintain independence and sense of self when physically becoming weaker, dependent on and fearing control by others
Independence variable, sometimes economic restrictions	How to maintain independence/sense of self	How to regain independence/sense of self		Minimal formal education*

Free time/leisure	Less time/little space/little money	New ground, interests; catching up education-ally; building confidence; achievement in change	Potential for personal change/new interests	Less access to educational provision; have time – lack money and mobility; physical debilities

NEEDS

Work-related training, continuing education and qualifications, specialised interests	Child-care, low fees, daytime classes, local centres; education – domestic vocational or liberal	Returning to educa-tion, work training, qualifications, special-ised and new interests	Survival skills, liberal studies	Easy access, daytime classes, low fees, social facilities and transport

* This will change by the twenty-first century as adults should be better educated when they reach pensionhood.

Notes

1 There are certain areas of survival and social skills which could be needed at any time in the lifecycle.
2 Women do not retire totally – maybe from low paid work but not from domestic ties and responsibilities.
3 Women with disabilities, depending on age and specific needs, can fit into this schematic model at all points, if facilities and opportunities are provided.

educational contact since many women take part in all kinds of informal learning through friendship networks, reading, talking, television, and interest groups (see also Chapter 2:39).

Notes

1 Personal communication from Sue Sharpe, 1983.
2 But see the monograph by Berryman, Julia C., 1981, *Sex Differences in Behaviour: Their Relevance for Adult Educators*: University of Nottingham, which provides a useful introductory review of some of the literature and its relevance to the learning needs of women and men, but little on identity.
3 Byrne, Eileen: 1978, *Women and Education*, Tavistock; Deem, Rosemary: 1978, *Women and Schooling*, Routledge & Kegan Paul; Eynard, Rosie and Walkerdine, Valerie: 1981, *Girls and Mathematics: The Practice of Reason*, University of London Institute of Education; Kelly, Alison: 1978, *Girls and Science: an International Study of Sex Differences in Science Achievement*, Almquist & Wiksell, Stockholm; Kelly, Alison: 1981, *The Missing Half, Girls and Science Education*, Manchester University Press; McRobbie, Angela: 1978, 'Working Class Girls and the Culture of Femininity' in *Women Take Issue*, Women's Studies Group, Centre for Contemporary Cultural Studies, University of Birmingham; Hutchinson, Enid: 1978, *Learning Later*, Routledge & Kegan Paul; Spender, Dale and Sarah Elizabeth: 1980, *Learning to Lose: Sexism and Education*, Women's Press; Spender, Dale and Sarah Elizabeth; 1982, *Invisible Women: The Schooling Scandal*, Writers and Readers; Sutherland, Margaret B.: 1981, *Sex Bias in Education*, Blackwell; Wolpe, Anne-Marie: 1977, *Some Processes in Sexist Education*, WRRC, London.
4 We have found the following works helpful: Ardener, Shirley: 1978, *Defining Females*, Croom Helm; Chetwynd, June and Hartnett, Oonagh: 1978, *The Sex Role System*, Routledge & Kegan Paul; Dinnerstein, Dorothy: 1976, *The Mermaid and the Minotaur*, Harper & Row; Gilligan, Carol: 1982, *In a Different Voice*, Harvard University Press; Hartnett, Oonagh, Boden, Gill and Fuller, Mary: 1979, *Sex-Role Stereotyping*, Tavistock Publications; Lipshitz, Susan (ed.): 1978, *Tearing the Veil*, Routledge & Kegan Paul; Miller, Jean Baker: 1973, *Psychoanalysis and Women*, Penguin Books; Mitchell, Juliet: 1974, *Psychoanalysis and Feminism*, Allen Lane; Rosaldo, R.Z. and Lamphere, L. (eds.) 1974, *Women, Culture and Society*, Stanford University Press. On the problems of doing feminist research in the social sciences, some useful books are: Roberts, Helen, 1981, *Doing Feminist Research*, Routledge & Kegan Paul; Stanley, Liz and Wise, Sue: 1983, *Breaking Out*, Routledge & Kegan Paul; and McRobbie, Angela: 1982, 'The Politics of Feminist Research: Between Talk, Text

and Action', in *Feminist Review*, no. 12: 46-57.

5 We were introduced to Hélène Cixous' work in a London Extra-Mural Class on French Feminism, Summer 1983, by the co-tutors, Clare Duchen and Clare Pajackowska.

6 See James Robertson's interesting ideas on relationships and work in the post industrial society in an article 'The Future of Work: Some Thoughts About the Roles of Men and Women in the Transition to a She Future' in *Women's Studies International Quarterly*, vol. 4, no. 1: 1981: 83-94.

Chapter 2
Women's Education –
Women's Studies

The women's liberation movement has given a voice to and created space for women together to discover and articulate their knowledge, oppressions and suppressions, guilts, angers and uncertainties in a co-operative and non-judgmental spirit. The release of energies, the raising of consciousness and the practice of starting from women's experience – 'the personal is political' – has begun to make visible the values of women and their ways of doing and being. In their practice women have shown that much can be achieved without the paraphernalia of institutional committees, minutes, standing orders, procedural matters, the pecking order of hierarchies, for these things hinder change and reform. Well-known examples are the rape crisis centres, the battered women's refuges and the Greenham Common peace women.

Sometimes it is easier to describe the influence of the women's liberation movement rather than the movement itself. It means different things to different women in different places at different times of different generations and from different cultures and classes. But it has one common thread which is its feminist consciousness. To define feminism is difficult, complex and controversial and would need several theses to explain. Our own working definition is that:

  (i) it pertains to women, including the social and psychological aspects of womanhood as distinct from the seemingly fixed biological aspects;

 (ii) it is an acute state of awareness about the nature and experiences of being a woman;

(iii) at different times in history and for different groups of women it has become visible in public struggles over equal rights, emancipation, birth control and sexuality, liberation and sisterhood. Activities around these and other issues create the feminist women's movements of the time;

(iv) feminists have different ideas and ways of achieving the freeing of women depending on their class, race, education and political perspectives.

The women's liberation movement is something like a kaleido-scope with interlinking moving centres and segments, which are constantly changing and reforming; they look different and of differing importance depending on how you perceive the pattern, and from where and when you look. Sometimes even feminists themselves have forgotten the need to keep focussing the kaleidoscope and to recognise different views and viewpoints. No one would dream of describing mankind by a single fixed phrase. So it is surely ludicrous to try to define women or the women's liberation movement with a single, negative catch-phrase (bra-burners, man-haters, women's-libbers. . .). Its influence is much wider than the numbers of feminists actively involved. Like most new ideas and movements which challenge and upset the accepted beliefs of their time, many of the ideas of the women's liberation movement, so radical yet timely when first formulated, are becoming widely known. Eventually they will be incorporated into the general social fabric. Freud's theories, for example, were considered disgraceful and subversive at first; now they are a part of our cultural background even if not acceptable to everybody.

We doubt that there is one adult in this country who has not heard of the women's liberation movement, even if only to joke about it. The women's liberation movement has, in other words, acted as a catalyst which has set off a reaction of profound questioning of patriarchal society which cannot be ignored, even though it may be hated and feared by those who hold power and privilege. Feminists' efforts have broken through the conspiracies of silence about issues such as housewives do work (unpaid); women do talk, not gossip – and not as much as men (Spender: 1980: 42); that rape and child molestation are both male violence; that wives as well as children are battered; that most women are concentrated in low-status, low-paid servicing jobs; that single parents are not immoral people; and that lesbians and gays have rights. Even women who strenuously maintain that they are not 'women's libbers' have in fact benefited from the courage, hard work and determination of women active in the women's liberation movement. They have gained confidence to begin to voice their needs and feelings in the home, in the workplace, in the trade unions, in churches and clubs, over issues such as equal pay for equal works, childcare, taxation, peace and abortion. The demand is for a re- vision of society and of culture (see Callaway: 1981: 457-71): not a fitting in, not an adding on, nor a putting back of women into the existing world.

In education, the influence and practices of the women's liberation movement has shaken the system and the curriculum. It is fairly commonplace now to refer to the women's liberation movement as a learning experience. The most obvious effect has been the generation and development of women's studies, which differ from the customary provision of education for women.

There has been much debate over whether women's studies are a separate academic discipline, or whether they have merely a consciousness-raising (CR) role within existing disciplines. Originally women's studies began in the existing disciplines (history or sociology, for example) but it was found impossible to discover or understand the complexities of why women were subordinate or left out without a comparative explanation of their position and the attitudes towards them in society at different periods. This entailed drawing upon the research and knowledge of disciplines like anthropology, sociology, psychology, the sciences, religious cultures, economics, legal systems, etc. They have re-ordered subject disciplines in an inter-disciplinary way and from a different perspective which have evolved into a new academic discipline. Women's studies draw upon, as well as re-interpreting, academically respected research.

But they are controversial not only because they are new, but also because they are asking different questions, devising new ways of research which lead to new forms of knowledge, and inevitably to the challenge of existing academic boundaries. The introduction of a new subject discipline into the universities in the past – economics, history, literature, sociology and psychology – met with similar resistance from the traditionalists in classics, law and medicine, philosophy and theology. One of the problems provoking resistance is that women's studies, being inter-disciplinary, are considered to be a dilution, even a pollution, of the purity of existing established subject areas.

Women's studies move away from the deficit model of women as lesser men as they allow women to create knowledge together rather than just receive it. They are indeed hard to pin down since the content will continue to evolve as research and time reveal fresh knowledge leading to new and changing perceptions and interpretations. So women's studies/feminist studies question and alter not only the given content of knowledge and ideas, but also provide a space for women in which the process of such discovery and learning builds up their confidence and the empowering of themselves. (Case studies Nos 4, 12, 13, 14, 16, 17 and 18 are examples of this process.)

We believe that there will always need to be a separate women's studies component to act as the powerhouse and conscience of all education. Otherwise there is the recurrent danger that women, having got so far in rediscovering and making their own ideas/knowledge/culture, will once again be submerged and have to struggle to recreate it afresh in each generation. This is both a waste of energy and time, as well as holding women back from new creative thought and work; it keeps women trapped at the level of angry frustration. Women's studies/feminist studies need to achieve an influence beyond their boundaries if education is to change. Feminism is not a marginal issue but one that profoundly affects all human kind.

> Women's studies . . . have already shown that they can enrich both scholarship and social policy demonstrating the dynamic force in the development of new forms of knowledge . . . programmes for teaching and research in women's studies are one of the means to secure women's complete equality. (UNESCO: 1980: 1)

This must include, of course, a rethinking of the meaning of equality. Women's studies will keep feminist ideas, research and teaching actively visible within education as well as providing a space and place for women to study together with feminist tutors, since women, coming from behind men, need the time on their own to work out in study together who they are, what they want, and how they are going to change society. It is unlikely that even sympathetic males will easily be able to forgo their deep-rooted male-centred opinions and ideas: they tend to see women's studies as the study of women or women's oppression, but women's studies are more than this. They are based on and include the experience of being a woman and part of a subordinate colonised majority/minority. So we do not think men could teach feminist studies to women but they can and should take on the study of gender and sex roles and relationships throughout the curriculum. They should study and teach what the implications of a feminist perspective are for them. (See Chapter 4, p. 158 for a reference to men's studies.)

But while we argue for the vital necessity and importance of maintaining a separate women's studies or feminist component within education to provide a feminist perspective in all subjects and all learning, we think it unrealistic that all women's education should or could be separated from the mainstream. The weakness of such a solution would be a marginalisation by men again of women's education within the old separate-but-equal argument, where women could exclusively and harmlessly pursue their studies, but men would continue to control their resources and remain untouched, unchanged by the feminist perspective.

Women have always been studied in a variety of contexts – mainly by men – but women's studies only emerged in the late 1960s out of the ideas and influence of the women's liberation movement. Women had learnt from the experience and practice of the black power movement in the United States that in order to understand the roots of and the reason for their subordinate position it was necessary to study without the presence of men. There were the women-only consciousness-raising (CR) groups which explored the common experience of being women. There was the work done by women around specific issues – health, the media, sexism in education and children's books, paid work and housework, and feminist history; and there were also the special campaigns, notably for equal opportunities legislation, nursery and childcare provision, the National Abortion Campaign (NAC), and Women's Aid (refuges for battered women). From such groups and work came some of the material which formed part of the content of the contemporary study of women within women's studies classes.

At the same time there were other influences affecting the universities which arose from the New Left, and sociology in particular, which raised questions about culture and working-class history; for example some universities set up new inter-disciplinary schools (as at Birmingham and Sussex). There also began to be demands from students that classes on women be included within their formal course work. Inside and outside the universities, women began to do research on the construction of femininity, the family in history and society, the sexual divisions within psychology and sociology, women in art and literature, girls and women in science and maths, and comparative cross-cultural studies of the family. This work was disseminated through networks such as conferences, women's journals, pamphlets and publishing, seminars and study groups, and especially through the Workers' Educational Association (WEA) and university adult education classes.

Of course there are tensions over the problem of making feminist research and the teaching of their findings academically acceptable. This, combined with the demands of academic institutions for measurable standards and formal examinations, conflicts with the spontaneity of the women's liberation movement at the grass roots. (The contradiction of how can you examine or grade what the experience of being a women is like!) In adult education the problem has not been so acute because of its flexibility; interdisciplinary studies suit the interests and needs of mature students and there are few examinations that have to be formally assessed. Part of the confusion over education for women arises from the terminology used to describe it. The term 'women's education' has normally been used to describe the so-called traditional provision, meaning in a large part domestic crafts and skills, physical activities, mainly offered by the local education authority (LEA) sector and some voluntary women's organisations such as the National Federation of Women's Institutes (WI), Townswomen's Guild (TG), the Co-operative Women's Guild (CWG) and Young Women's Christian Association (YWCA). We would argue that this definition obscures the issue, since women's education is much broader than just educating women to continue within their traditional roles. All education for women, including what generically is called women's studies/feminist studies, should come under the umbrella term of women's education.

We suggest that there are four major strands in women's education which are broad enough and varied enough to embrace all types of foreseen need. These are particularly appropriate to adult education.

(i) The extension of traditional so-called women's subjects which are usually domestically orientated; the opening up of traditional, so-called male subjects to make them relevant and appropriate to women – car maintenance, carpentry, computers, electronics, mathematics and navigation courses.

(ii) Education that is positive discrimination to make up for the fact that girls and women generally receive less education and training than boys and men, and also because the existing provision does not fit the lifecycles and needs of women.

(iii) Classes for women about women which both rediscover women's lives and achievements, use feminist research and raise awareness about re-visioning the world and women's place in it.

(iv) Ensuring that there is a feminist dimension and that women are actively visible in all adult education courses and classes. This means a study of gender in the curriculum, that is in all subjects and courses.

(See also Hughes and Kennedy: 1983: 266 where we first suggested these distinctions.)

(i) Extending traditional subjects (as differentiated from (iv) below)

A major part of local education authority (LEA) adult education programmes consist of cookery, fashioncrafts and beauty care. Such courses should not only have their art/craft/skill element raised in status, but women should be made aware of the bias behind these subjects. There is the assumption that skills are always neutral. They could and should be extended to include, for example, an analysis of the dynamics of the cultural and class basis of cookery and fashioncrafts; an examination of why women feel the need to make themselves more attractive, as well as understanding the chemical properties and possible side-effects of beauty care products, and the environmental and economic questions involved in producing and marketing them. Such approaches would encourage *thinking*, rather than just the compliant acceptance of taught and received knowledge (Hughes and Kennedy: 1983: 266). Whereas it is necessary to extend and develop the curriculum in the traditional women's subjects, it is also essential to give women access to subject areas normally dominated by men. This means at the practical level a change in attitudes: having female as well as male tutors, encouraging the equal participation of women and men, and making the language and teaching examples relevant to women's experience. But women may also need and want to study such subjects in women-only groups in ways that are specifically appropriate to themselves, not because they are deficient, but because they have not been allowed access to practical male experience and knowledge. For example:

(a) *Women and Manual Trades* (WAMT) which was started in 1975 by a few women working in the building industry who wanted to share work experiences, as well as give each other advice and support. It now includes women working in trades such as welding, masonry, gardening, mechanics and engineering, as well as carpentry and joinery, plumbing, painting and decorating, electrics, bricklaying and plastering. Since then it has worked with other women's employment groups, in campaigns about childcare facilities, flexible working hours, and women-only training, and have lobbied training agencies and unions. The group visits schools, runs practical workshops and introductory courses for women and girls, and provides a national support network. (See WAMT publicity leaflet: 1983.)

(b) *The East Leeds Women's workshop*, which began in June 1982 with funding from the European Social Fund and Leeds City Council, offers facilities for up to sixty women a year to train in electronics, microcomputing, carpentry and joinery. There are both full- and part-time courses. The most innovative aspect of the project is that there is free childcare provision. The workshop does not have a crèche, but places have been obtained for the under-fives in local social services day nurseries. In addition there is a collection service from local schools, after-school care and very good holiday play schemes. This is very different from the experience of the Deptford Skill Centre (See Case Study No. 10).

One of the most interesting examples of ways in which women can make visible a subject area which was not considered by the experts and authorities to be valid educationally or a suitable subject for women is *women's self-defence courses*. The establishment of such courses for women in London posed many problems. Previously self-defence was linked to the martial arts which were seen as a traditionally male preserve. When women's self-defence groups,[1] because of the violence against women on city streets, began to want the training and philosophy they had developed together to be widely available to all women, there seemed no way that the existing structures and regulations of the Inner London Education Authority (ILEA) could respond. The Authority, on the advice of the College of Physical Education, took the view that this was solely a physical activity demanding tutors with black or brown belts from one of the four recognised martial arts. Not surprisingly few women have these qualifications. There was little recognition that self-defence covers far more than just learning to respond physically to violence. The women's self-defence groups have developed an inter-disciplinary approach where they combine the teaching of physical techniques with experiental learning that draws upon discussion among students about their own experiences and attitudes. The class focusses on students' own strategies, mental, physical and verbal, for avoiding violence and for dealing with it if it cannot be avoided; even joking your way out of a situation or using dirty tricks can be appropriate.

After repeated requests for classes, and pressure from many quarters (women's self-defence groups, women in the Inner London Education Authority and the Workers' Educational Association, community education workers and politicians), two contrasting pilot classes were put on. This was followed by a day conference in March 1982 which made policy recommendations: that women's self-defence is a subject in its own right under the Women's Studies Inspector and not the Physical Education Inspectorate; the first batch of tutors had to be validated, ready to teach in the 1982 autumn term. New prospective tutors come together for training and study with women experienced in self-defence, and together, working in small supportive groups, define their own individual training needs. As a group they decide whether individuals within it are ready to teach, to become co-tutors, or that more training would be helpful. (See also ILEA *Contact*: 7 May 1982: 11.) Once these self-defence classes became established in the London adult education institutes the demand for them could not be met. This indicates that women as well as educators are not always aware of what their needs are until the provision is made overt – put in the programme.[2]

(ii) Education that is positive discrimination

This encompasses a variety of provision, starting at different levels of need to reach out and draw in women of all classes and lifestyles. The courses range from literacy to diplomas in management studies. The example of the way in which, from the early 1970s, the part-time tutors, who were predominantly women, worked together on developing the newly perceived needs of adults in literacy, numeracy, basic life skills, and English as a Second Language (ESL), have implications for women's education. The tutors developed their own teaching materials for adults, and taught on a one-to-one or small-group basis. In working out their policies in a democratic, non-hierarchical way, they put pressure on adult education institutions in the process to positively discriminate in favour of these new kinds of courses by diverting more funds, space and support to them: low or no fees, the provision of crèches, more teaching hours. (Case Study No. 2 shows, however, that more men than women take advantage of this kind of provision because it is still not sufficiently geared to the needs of women.)

Some women will move on from literacy classes into courses with similar aims but with a variety of names: New Opportunities for Women (NOW) (see Case Study No. 18), Fresh Horizons, Fresh Start, Breakaway (see Case Study No. 4), Return-to-Study, Access, and Second Chance – the last two are particularly for working-class women and men (see Case Study No. 12) – are just some of the better-known names. Since their introduction from the mid-1960s they have offered women, in particular, some positive opportunities for a re-evaluation of their educational needs and the prospect of further study or re-entry into the job market. Although, as Alice Lovell pertinently points out, the time-scale for women coming from one of these courses and going on to higher education might mean that they are too old to enter graduate training schemes in the Civil Service or large industrial concerns (Lovell: 1980: 100-103). Women are discriminated against institutionally by both age and sex. For other women, who, for whatever reason, do not take their education further, these courses can be invigorating, mind-expanding, and give them new confidence in their intellectual and social abilities which can be beneficial to themselves, their families and the community. (See also Hutchinson: 1978; Mace, Moss & Snee: 1982; Michaels and Booth: 1979; Storey and Reid: 1980, for a fuller discussion on these kinds of courses.)

Hillcroft College, the only residential government-funded college for adult women in the UK,[3] has a long history of providing education for women, many without formal qualifications. Recently it has begun to move away from its traditional Oxbridge curriculum. The lecture-tutorial system is being extended by more small-group work, and study skills are now compulsory in the first year, as these are more particularly valuable to mature women learners. New options in drama and computer studies have been introduced into the two-year certificate courses in Social Sciences or Combined Studies. Whereas in the past students were expected to stay for two years, now they can be encouraged to leave after one year if they know where they want to go or what they want to do. At the same time the college has begun to open up its facilities to the local community by offering short courses. One particularly innovative approach has been 'Valuing Your Experience'; this gives women the opportunity to review, assess and build on their experiences, however ordinary or unimportant they feel them to be.[4] This educational process has been developed in this country by the New Directions for Older Women group whose philosophy concentrates on women's strengths – what they enjoy doing and what they do well in their lives so that each woman can recognise, value and act upon her talents (see Musgrove and Mennell: 1980). Such an approach links in with the methods and intentions of assertion training classes which are rapidly growing in popularity in the Local Education Authority (LEA) sector and the Workers' Educational Association (WEA). (For a fuller account see Dickson: 1982.)

For those women based in the home the Open University provides, with its distance learning study methods and a modular credit system, one type of higher education that fits neatly into the fragmented pattern of women's lives. It seems that this positive and relevant model, with its open access, which was established to provide education for those who had not been able to attend universities or polytechnics – this was assumed to be the working class – has been eagerly taken up by women. The number of female students has grown remarkably from 5,300 out of 19,600 in 1970/71 to 30,100 out of 67,700 in 1981/82. The percentage of students who defined themselves as housewives grew from 10 per cent to 18 per cent in the same ten years (*Social Trends* no. 13: 1983: 445). It is often forgotten that housewives are an underprivileged group in terms of education.[5] (See also Case Study No. 19 for an analysis of how the Open University was reluctant to recognise Women's Studies as an academic subject.)

(iii) Women/feminist studies – classes for women about women

The first known women's studies course in Britain was run by Juliet Mitchell at the anti-university in 1968-9. Since then they have formed a part of some degree and diploma courses in the majority of British universities and polytechnics, but so far there are only a few higher education institutions which offer specific degree qualifications in women's studies (Bradford, Kent, London, York, Sheffield, and diplomas at Goldsmith College and the Polytechnic of Central London). The main developments have been within adult education, especially in the Workers' Educational Association (WEA) and university adult education departments, and now the Local Education Authorities (LEAs). There are no figures available as to the extent and number of women's studies classes in Britain but it is widely recognised that there has been a considerable growth in these because of the controversies and debates they have aroused within adult education. (See Case Studies Nos 15 and 19 for fuller accounts of the difficulties and controversies.)[6]

The example of developments within the Extra-Mural Department of London University shows how, in the last ten years, courses have not only grown in numbers but have changed in emphasis; from 3 or 4 in 1973/4 with general titles (Women and the Cinema, Women and/or Literature) to 12 classes in 1978/9 still with all-embracing titles (Women in Society, Women in History, etc.) to 28 in 1983/4 indicating more specialised study (Autobiography; Women and Writing; Feminism and Film; Sex, Love and Friendship; Beginning in the Middle – a workshop for older women; Psychoanalysis and Female Identity; Research and Resources in Feminist History). This shows how women's studies in one place have grown in both confidence and knowledge.

In the United States by contrast the growth of women's studies has been well documented because the majority of courses take place within universities and colleges. In 1983 there were over 30,000 individual women's studies courses, and over 430 institutions of higher education offering 130 BA courses as well as 45 MA and 10 PhD programmes. There were also 28 women's research centres compared with 2 in the United Kingdom (Duelli-Klein: 1984). Even allowing for the population difference, where the United States outnumbers the United Kingdom in a rough proportion of four to one, the growth in women's studies in the United States has been remarkable.

Apart from the more academically based women's studies courses there has been the recent development of classes, within women's studies, which help women to survive and develop. These include assertion training, self-defence, women's rights, housing and employment, and many kinds of self-help courses, as well as writing and history workshops. There will often be a feminist element within some of the positive discrimination courses such as Fresh Horizons, Second Chance and Return-to-Study as well.

At the moment women's studies courses, like all other adult education classes, are open by law to everyone.[7] An unresolved problem remains because although the majority of students are women, there are times when a few men join the classes. This can be particularly difficult, even destructive, when subjects such as women's sexuality or health are being studied. There is a need for women-only classes (see Case Study No. 19 which reflects some of the difficulties of getting this view accepted); and also for men to

organise their own men's studies. The debate over women-only
classes still remains confused. Some authorities and institutions
allow these classes if there are comparable classes being offered
generally to men. This still creates a difficulty for the development
of new types of classes for women because often there is nothing
comparable for men. The problem would of course be helped if
there was a feminist dimension in all education. (For a fuller
examination of the debates around women's studies see Bowles and
Duelli Klein: 1983; the articles in *Women's Studies International Forum*:
1983: vol. 6, no. 3; and in *Feminist Review*, nos 14 and 15: 1983.)

(iv) A feminist dimension in all education

If the world is truly going to change then there must be a feminist
dimension and the study of gender in all levels of education. This
means a changed perspective in the teaching, study and organisation of all courses and classes. Men will have to change their
perspectives as well, because it is not just a tacking on of women –
putting them back into history or taking them out of dress-making
– but it entails the opening up of every subject of study to include
women, children, the old, people from different races. In education
this would mean beginning with educating the staff and not only
the students – a reversal of assumptions and roles which may be
hard for a tutor and administrator to accept at first. Acknowledg-
ing gender as well as race has to be an integral part in the
transformation of all knowledge and teaching. Different standards
for and judgments of minority women have often meant lower
standards and they are usually expected to conform and integrate
on white terms. Little attention or respect is given to their
knowledge of story-telling, cookery, music, work and family roles.
The majority of minority women employed in adult education at
present are canteen workers, cleaners, creche assistants or
secretaries; they are rare as tutors.

The difficulty is that because women are spread through all
classes and locked into relationships with men at home and at
work, men are unaware of or do not wish to know about the
imbalance in the power division between women and men. At work
men are the bosses; at home they are the head of the household; in
education they are the directors. Most men would say that they are
caring and concerned individuals who do things for the good of
their workforce, their family and their students (benevolent
paternalism). It is in fact somewhat easier to get men to face the

issues of racism, because it touches their social and historical conscience, rather than confront their own sexism. Ultimately we can neither expect or trust even a concerned dominant group to make the changes that would fundamentally redistribute the power it holds.

It seems to us that in adult education there is a need to learn some practices from the women's liberation movement and to set up discussion-awareness groups for staff development which begin to break down the hierarchical relationships and silences. Most of us who work in the field of education for adults do a multiplicity of jobs, because the service is under-resourced, under-housed and under-staffed. In fact the adult educator's working life is as fragmented as any woman's. But there is still an underlying system of power and control. For example a responsive and involved secretary will do a lot of informal counselling and advice work which is hardly ever recognised by the system. Likewise a canteen worker or the caretaker play as important a role as the more highly esteemed and paid tutor or organiser in relating to the students.

It is difficult to give concrete examples of how women's experience, knowledge and views of the world should be implemented in every aspect of education, since the ground is being newly furrowed. The following suggestions, however, show ways in which gender could be introduced. It means starting from a different angle and using new hypotheses. It could be an archaeology class where the concept of the gatherer is given equal importance to that of the hunter; a writing class where the reader's experience is as valid as the author's; a chemistry class which analyses the baking properties of bread; an interior design course which examines the home as a functional place of work, not just as an aesthetic living space; a class on family law which studies the moral and social climate in which the laws were introduced; courses on film which discuss how women are depicted, or the process of how films are constructed, or the way the film industry works; pre-retirement courses which recognise that women never retire; parent education which emphasises that women and *men* are parents. Education cannot remain static since it is a continuous process which shifts and changes as ideas and knowledge, which have always been there unacknowledged, are dug up and revealed.

This can be illustrated by the changing processes of women's struggles in the twentieth century. Initially it was a struggle for the 'vote', the emancipation of women. This did not bring the hoped-for equality since legal, social and economic positions did not shift enough actually to give women real equality (work, pay, responsibility for children, the wife's financial dependency and so on). The next stage was a recognition that changing the man-made structures was neither easy nor adequate; attitudes had to change as well if women, and men, were to be liberated from their conventional roles and prejudices.

If education is to be both relevant and enhancing of life and living, it should not be compartmented into subject boxes. It should assume an inter-disciplinary approach which better relates to adult experience and changing lifestyles at different ages and stages of personal and work cycles. Much of the work and knowledge discovered or rediscovered in women's studies could be carried over into educational generally. This does not necessarily mean that only a feminist tutor can do this; it has to be made a part of every tutor's educational baggage. The major part of any education programme, in theory, is aimed at both women and men, and yet the knowledge studied has a prevailing masculine bias. It is not just a question of modifying 'men's studies', generally known as universal knowledge, but of operating on and correcting the stigmatism. The following example shows the classic assumptions that continue to be prevalent about women's and men's roles.

> The reduction in the length of the working week has meant that more and more time has become available for leisure activities. One hundred and fifty years ago a man might expect to work a six-day week, and each shift might last from dawn to dusk. Today the four day working week is a possibility and few shifts last longer than eight hours. Similar changes have taken place in *the lives of people who do not work – the housewife* for example. (our italics: Nixon: 1977)[8]

This is a value judgment which cannot be substantiated in real life, since women do work in the family, but until recent years such work, because unpaid, was invisible and unacknowledged. Furthermore, if a feminist perspective is rightly included in all education, it is just as necessary that class, age, race and other biases and omissions should also be tackled within the curriculum. Whilst this would obviously be of prime importance to those who have been classified as 'disadvantaged', it also means that men will be learning a totally different kind of knowledge where they will not necessarily be, either implicitly or explicitly, the dominant and most-studied creatures.

Curriculum changes alone will not work without genuine and open access to the institutions themselves. For example, the recent campaign within the Workers' Educational Association (WEA) by the Women's Education Advisory Committee for childcare facilities for all classes led to a National Conference in the autumn of 1982 to explore the issues. A model creche was funded by the Equal Opportunities Commission (EOC); a pamphlet on how to set up and fund creches was available; and for the first time it was agreed to have a creche for the biennial national conference. Just a few years ago such an event would not have been considered educationally important and children would have remained the sole responsibility of the mother or parent. It is vital for educators to maintain antennae that are sensitive and powerful enough to pick up and interpret the signals being transmitted from different directions and levels. The resultant programmes of all kinds, from the experiential, feminist, personal, political, practical, radical, separatist and the traditional should not be jammed or intercepted by those who operate the controls.

Beyond the formal

Probably most of us are not fully aware of how much informal learning goes on all the time throughout our lives. People do not see this as proper education since that is always associated with being inside schools, colleges and centres, and being taught, monitored and controlled. We should observe and give credit to the ways women go about educating themselves, be it swopping cookery recipes, do-it-yourself activities, reading a book, watching television, running a playgroup, organising a jumble sale, gardening, and so on. Women also participate in all kinds of other activities in the community which provide informal learning in different sorts of ways; these remain largely unrecorded. For example, community and tenants' associations; choral, drama and music societies; church groups, some sports clubs; local history, archaeology and environmental societies; the peace movements; single-issue pressure groups like the Child Poverty Action Group, the political parties and the trade unions. Of course these are often mixed groups, but some of them do have separate women's sections which are the unequal half of the whole. Women can and do act as the conscience of their wider movements or associations according to the level of consciousness of their status and role at particular times. This has an educative impact, but does not necessarily change the power relationship between women and men, or only slowly and reluctantly. However, pressure has made the Trades

Union Congress (TUC) aware of homeworkers and child care needs, the abortion issue and women's under-representation on union executives and committees. It is true that trade unions are still slow to move towards flexible job sharing, equal pay and women's rights with men to employment. Whilst political parties pay lip service to equality, there are fewer women members of Parliament (3 per cent) today than there were in 1964; and at the local level there are on average four men to every woman councillor (Cousins: 1981).

For some women their involvement and work in voluntary or community organisations gives them the power, status and influence which they would rarely achieve through the traditional channels which are open to men – career, jobs, churches, political parties and the trade unions. It is often assumed that this is done by women who have some kind of financial support. But this is not entirely the case: groups to do with holiday, nursery or play facilities for children, tenants' and residents' action associations, co-operatives, the Claimants' Union, Mothers in Action (1965-1975), and a variety of education and health pressure groups, amongst many other examples, have been activated and led by local working-class women. Despite their abilities and initiatives, they are so often used as the supporting cast in many mixed organisations, even if they are competent to take the lead, the star role. Authority is still seen to be more effective if it is invested in the male.

Of course women can see and do things differently, but in reality they seem to get caught inside bodies that are hierarchically organised. There are some cases where power is shared in a more open and democratic way. The National Abortion Campaign (NAC) has shown in its campaigns to preserve the 1967 Abortion Reform Act that it was able to work effectively with organisations such as the British Medical Association (BMA), the Abortion Law Reform Association (ALRA), the Trades Union Congress (TUC) and the women's liberation movement. The National Council for Civil Liberties (NCCL) is another example where women have made the organisation aware of the issues which affect women's liberties as well as new ways of working both within and outside the organisation.

All this informal do-it-yourself education goes on in spite of the fact that women have far less clearly demarcated leisure time than men. This is partly because women's lives are fragmented – split into many different jobs, cares and responsibilities which spill over into women's time and also because unpaid homemaking duties are not seen as real work. So there is a less clear demarcation between where their work time ends and their leisure (free time) begins, since leisure is defined as non-work-time or non-obligated time which applies more appropriately to men in employment. It is apparent that both women and men do not see a clear distinction between women's working times and their 'spare' time. (Of course women who do paid jobs, working outside the home, caring for the family and being a homemaker, have even less leisure time.) Many women feel obliged to use most of their non-sleeping time in useful tasks around the household. Even when sitting down to watch television they may well be sewing, darning socks or knitting, and family and public holidays (leisure time for men and children, especially boys) mean extra work for most women. Thus women's learning and leisure is more homebound than men's. Such informal learning for them often comes from the social groups to which they belong, from family and friendship networks, from radio and television (see also p. 149, where women watched the BBC Computer literacy programmes in the privacy of their homes rather than going out to study in classes on computing). Unlike men who have more money, more time free of work, can walk the streets more safely and can meet more acceptably as individuals in club or pub, women's lives are more circumscribed by physical and conventional restrictions.

Yet, despite these constraints, women are the main participants in adult education classes as well as being active in many organisations. Still they remain invisible, unheard from wherever they stand. Formal adult education should be a shell into which women and people can fit themselves, move around and use the educational fixtures and resources as they will.

Notes

1 There are women's self-defence groups in Birmingham, Brighton, Canterbury, Hull, Leeds, Liverpool, Manchester, Newcastle, Oxford and Sheffield, as well as in other places.
2 Another pertinent example comes from Norway. In the early 1970s, with the expansion of the oil fields, there was a skilled manpower shortage. Instead of recruiting and training migrant workers, women were offered the opportunity of training as welders, truck drivers, etc. They applied in great numbers although they had not previously demanded or been interested in such vocational training. This response caught the adult

education training agencies by surprise (Kallerud: 1980: 22).

3 At least 50 per cent of students came to Hillcroft because it is a women-only college. And in a recent survey (1983) of current students more than eight out of ten students wished it to remain so (*Times Higher Education Supplement*: 15 July 1983).

4 Interview with the Principal, Phoebe Lambert, July 1983.

5 The category of housewives includes those employed for less than twenty hours per week.

6 This is an area that is urgently in need of research (see Bradshaw et al.: *Women's Studies and Courses in the United Kingdom*: 1981).

7 It is possible to obtain an exemption for specifically designated courses for women only from the Department of Employment. These are only given for individual courses and not to the organisation as a whole and in practice the Department tend to favour training-type courses.

8 We are indebted to Rosemary Auchmuty for this quotation.

Chapter 3
Where Women are, and Where are Women in Adult Education?

> You said 'man' and 'he'
> But where were we?
> Women who hold up half the sky,
> You said 'man' and 'he'
> But where were we?
> We were invisible
> We were unheard
> And we know why.

(This chorus was composed in a women's workshop at the International Council of Adult Education Conference in Paris, October 1982)

Education, in common with many other institutions in our society, preaches a philosophy of change for the individual based on national, traditional and cultural values, whilst maintaining control of resources and curriculum. No aware person now would deny that in Britain we are living with a whole range of issues and changes whose outcome is uncertain. There is unrest and unemployment among the young; the population is ageing – currently more than eight million people are over 65 years (*Social Trends*: 1983: 13). The moral dilemmas and anguish around nuclear power and the question of peace deeply disturb people. There are the problems associated with painfully adjusting to being a multiracial society whilst having to come to terms with Britain's diminishing status as a former world power. The technological revolution will alter commonly accepted patterns of full-time work and employment. As a consequence leisure or free non-working time will become a reality. We are moving into a post-industrial society in the twenty-first century using nineteenth-century models. Yet policy-makers have been emotionally and educationally slow to adapt to these profound changes. Similarly the reluctance has been even greater to acknowledge that women are part of the human species, in fact more than half of it – and have always been here, although their presence has often been ignored or submerged. As Susan Griffin has described it:

> The events of our lives – childbirth, domestic labour, child raising, abortion, our sexual lives, rape, our work as secretaries, or nurses – faded into the background, as if these events had nothing to do with the social structure or politics or culture but rather were part of the landscape, the given existence. (Griffin: 1982: 6)

Education is particularly guilty of this erasure of women's lives. Even in adult education where the majority of staff and students are women, the teaching and class provision seems to be based on traditional cultural assumptions where men are the definers and doers, and women, like children, black people, the working class, the old and disabled are a subnormal species to be differently categorised, studied and provided for. All the cultural values are unquestionably male-defined and measured. It can be argued that this process is unconscious, 'natural' and not conspiratorial, and that cultural traditions are older than present customs. But they work out in practice to the advantage of men, and men quite understandably, as the sex that profits from such a system, have not been overly anxious to change radically these assumptions which are so beneficial to them.

If we take the family as one key component in education and culture, we now know from a huge body of research that there are many inconsistencies and tensions between the female and male perceptions and experiences of this important social and economic institution. Education is closely interrelated with the family and schooling, training for jobs, higher education and further education and the sorts of provision made for adults designed to reinforce the family as it exists. Family, for a man, means power as the ordained legal head of the household; the children bear his name, he has financial control as the predominant wage earner, free sex as of right, status and support for paid work outside the home. Within a usually monogamous and stable heterosexual relationship he receives care for his bodily needs, and affection for his emotional needs. Family, for a woman, means to become a wife, at best to assume nominal equality with her husband who is head of the household. It also means motherhood, a home, another name to take, an unpaid servicing job of household and emotional maintenance, and usually financial dependency. She is considered to be the emotional centre and supplier of affection and support for the whole family in return for protection, food and shelter. She is dependent and depended upon. And should she do paid work outside the home, in a low-paid sexually segregated job, which mirrors the sexual division of labour within the family, this does not give her great status. Her prime function in life is still considered to be married and have children. It is impossible for women and men to have equality within the family structure when the values and functions of one are prized more highly than the other's.

Furthermore, this description of a 'typical' family is belied by the reality, which shows a rather different picture. Only 5 per cent of households in Britain at any one time consists of the so-called normal family: a working father, a wife and mother at home looking after 2 (or rather 1.9) dependent children (General Household Survey: 1979). Other groupings and households consist of married couples without children or with children who have left home, single people and single-parent families. The majority of single-parent families are headed by women – 760,000 (compared with 100,000 by men) of whom 510,000 were either divorced or separated (National Council for One-Parent Families: 1979).[1] In addition to these traditional and accepted heterosexual patterns there has been a growth in other kinds of relationships and living arrangements such as lesbian and gay couples, others who have made a positive decision to remain childfree, and communal households. So families are changing, even if they were ever as 'normal' as they were assumed to be in the past. Although over 90 per cent of women today will be married at some time in their lives, the majority of divorce petitions are brought by women: 123,000 compared with 47,000 brought by men in 1981 (*Social Trends*: 1983: 31), one result of the 1970 Divorce Reform Act. This emergent divorce pattern does raise the question about whether marriage is not made by men for men rather than for women. Nowadays women do have somewhat more social and economic mobility than even twenty years ago. Their expectations have also changed; previously they would have felt it their duty to stay in a marriage, however unsatisfactory; now they feel entitled to leave. It is quite widely assumed that initially women are more in favour of marriage then men. Later, however, once the spouses have experienced marriage, the roles are often reversed: women want to extend their horizons beyond the front door whereas men become the preservers of the family institution. It is debatable how many of these changes, this dissatisfaction with marriage and family, are due to the climate of the times. Quite often this development is blamed upon easier access to contraception, particularly the pill, easier divorce, social security benefits, changing housing policies, the slow movement towards equal opportunities for women and the radical challenges and questions raised by the women's liberation movement – the second wave of feminism in twentieth-century Britain.

Marriage and the family have different educational implications for women and men. As the authors of a report on mature students in Ulster noted:

> ... the marriage-family institution tends to produce a dichotomy betwen men and women. It acts as an inhibition to women's career development, which for many women is final, and at the same time acts as a powerful support to men's career development. . . . So the notion must be promoted that for many women the years after 25 act as the equivalent of the time after 17 for men. . . (Morgan and Dunn: 1980: 73)

Not only for this reason, but also because girls often make limiting choices at school which restrict their later job and career opportunities, we want to see a genuine extension of education that is freely available to all people, but especially to girls and women at all stages in their life. The following quotation indicates a commonly held attitude towards education and the family: 'Educate a boy and you educate a person; educate a girl and you educate a family' (Crowcroft: 1983: 380).

This is one reason why the revived women's liberation movement of the 1970s concentrated its initial energies on an examination of the family and women's subordinate status within it:

> Much of the oppression of women takes place 'in private', in areas of life considered 'personal'. The causes of that oppression are social and economic but these causes could only be revealed and confronted when women challenged the assumptions of their personal life, of who does the housework, of the way children are brought up, the quality of our friendships, even the way we make love and with whom. These were not normally the subject of politics. (Rowbotham, Segal and Wainwright: 1981: 13)

It has been said that the women's liberation movement is a learning experience. Jack Mezirow has described this feminist approach to learning as 'the perspective transformation of knowledge'. Adult education could benefit from adopting some of these processes (Mezirow: 1977). Most women's groups begin as consciousness-raising (CR) meetings where women discuss and discover in a non-hierarchical and supportive setting their experience of living as women in a male-ordered society. This process of experiental learning, questioning and sharing knowledge usually expands beyond the inner circle of personal experience into either a more specialist analytical and theoretical study of women and society, or into an activist phase around community and women's issues. This concept of making and sharing knowledge is not alien to or unknown in adult education, hence, for example, the idea that has been attributed to Tawney that every Workers' Educational Association (WEA) class consists of 'thirteen tutors and thirteen students'. The ideal of tutor and students together negotiating their own areas of study reflects the ideas of shared responsibility inherent in feminism.

The work and ideas of Paulo Freire developed in the 1950s and 1960s in the rural areas of Brazil and Chile also have similarities to the learning processes of the women's liberation movement. His work in literacy evolved around a kind of education where the teacher and learners worked together to solve problems. This went beyond just learning to read and write because they drew upon their own experience to make the learning materials they used. The intention was to raise consciousness (conscientisation) about their oppression and develop an awareness that change is possible (see Freire: 1972a, 1972b). Although not feminist, Freire's emphasis on the value of experiental learning among rural peasants in the Third World is not dissimilar to the women's liberation movement's own practice.

It has recently been pointed out that experiental learning is not taken seriously by most educational institutions and validating bodies as a means of access to further or higher education. This particularly affects women, as well as working-class people, both of whom are less well qualified in a traditional sense, but they do have a varied experience of life and work which fits them for education if only this could be recognised.[2]

> it is the learning from experience that matters, not the experience itself. That distinction between experience and what has been learnt through experience is the beginning. Thus, to set out to assess experiental learning is to begin to reassess education itself. (Evans: 1983: 9)

This emphasis on learning from personal experience is crucial.

Such a new departure proposing the validity of experiential learning would obviously benefit women and others who have not progressed through the formal education structures. But it raises questions about what criteria would be used and who would evaluate the experiential learning itself.

Education for adults

The education of adults in the formal institutions is still dominated by two major strands: the transmission of the 'great tradition' of our cultural heritage, principally Euro-centred; and the idea of education as training within the nineteenth-century concept of 'useful knowledge'. In the latter, so-called neutral skills were taught to make people competent in the three Rs, domestic economy, carpentry, sewing, first aid, and physical fitness. Essentially this type of education works to maintain the status quo, and assumes that people should not rise above their allotted station in life. Interestingly Richard Johnson, in his study of popular working-class education and politics in the early nineteenth century, describes what 'really useful knowledge' meant to the working class. It was knowledge that was practical, decided by them and helped towards an understanding of 'a theory of exploitation in the economic realm, a theory of state power, a theory of cultural domination' (Johnson: 1979). Unfortunately, like most male researchers, he does not question the masculine assumptions behind this knowledge, but his research indicates how the different classes see the same thing, knowledge, in different ways. The same analogy can be made about feminist and other perceptions of knowledge today.

The emphasis on the great cultural tradition – art, literature, history, philosophy, some sciences, music and languages – allows students to study and participate in the dominant culture. This tends to develop an inherent respect for traditional values and an unquestioning belief in experts and authorities. Before the expansion of higher education in Britain after 1944 many people received most of their education and knowledge from the university extra-mural movement and the Workers' Educational Association (WEA). The diaries and records of working people, men in particular, reveal the excitement and frustration they found in coming into contact with this cultural tradition. There was a real belief that education could transform society (Roger Fieldhouse: 1977; J.F.C. Harrison: 1961; Sheila Rowbotham: 1981: 62-95).

Nevertheless the courses were and are usually comfortable rather than confrontational, in the best liberal traditions of 'balanced' presentation and rare obvious censorship, although controversial divisions of opinion and debate did and can still arise in classes on politics and sociology, for example. Yet what is rarely discussed is the tacit acceptance of many stereotypes that together form the ideology of the norm. We have already pointed up how women's and men's roles within the family and society at large are preserved.

It is worth remembering that discussion on politics and religion was prohibited by the rules of many Mechanics' Institutes in the first half of the nineteenth century. Similarly the government has tried to determine the political and social content of Youth Training Scheme courses. A draft memorandum (Summer 1983) by the Minister of Employment to the Manpower Services Commission states, 'Matters related to the organisation and functioning of society in general should be excluded unless they are relevant to trainees' experience' (*Guardian*: 11 October 1983). These two examples show how classes for working people or unemployed youth have been circumscribed by the fairly definite ideas of the providers on what is suitable educational material. This is a clear illustration of how a dominant group attempts to control the learning and behaviour of subordinate groups. (See also Case Studies nos 2 and 16 for accounts of attempts to censor teaching material.)

Similarly the insistence on gaining competence in the skills-based courses, even if this remained unstated, aimed at maintaining an efficient and compliant workforce. This emphasis on vocational skills and training applied equally to women and men. Women's 'natural' vocation was assumed to centre around childcare and domestic matters, even though this ignored the reality that the majority of working-class women worked for a wage outside the home. It is ironic that it was, and still is, considered necessary to teach women their 'natural' role and duties which one could surely assume they would know already as part of their feminine 'nature'. In so many ways the nineteenth-century tradition of 'separate spheres', and therefore separate educational provision for women and men, has been maintained today with the attendant differing values and status. As standards of living have improved, so the domestic subjects, forming roughly one-third of the total adult education provision (Mee and Wiltshire: 1978: 37) have tended toward icing the cake rather than baking it, e.g.

cordon bleu cookery, beauty care, designing clothes. This confirms women in arts and skills as ever-better homemakers. Today these skills-based classes tend to attract the better-off and socially aspiring women. At the other end of the social scale, particularly in urban areas, there is the development of what is, in essence, a means-tested education service for those labelled 'disadvantaged' or deemed to be deficient. While formerly the emphasis was on literacy and numeracy, it has now been extended into adult basic education, which attempts to give people the life skills to survive in a complex and confusing society. It is important to recognise the many ways in which adult education supports the existing family structures – parent education, home visiting schemes, family studies and child development classes. It does not seem to have responded, to any great extent so far, to issues like alternative lifestyles, changing sex roles, gender identity or new evolving family patterns.

One of the contradictions of the formal adult education service, as Nell Keddie has so pertinently pointed out, is that although it is 'a women's service' – studented in the main by women, serviced by women – it is run by men (Keddie 1981: unpublished paper). In 1982 there were 1,534,000 students in adult education and youth centres in England, of whom 1,000,585 (65%) were women. This does not include those adults who attend classes in colleges of further education. There were 173,682 adults studying in university extra-mural departments of whom 100,585 (58%) were women and 122,001 adults attending Workers' Educational Association (WEA) classes; 72,438 of the latter were women representing 59% of the total. It is ironic to note that of the 1,080 students attached to the Welsh National Council of the Young Men's Christian Association, 835 (77%) were women (DES statistics: 1982).

This disturbing state of affairs belies a much-believed assumption that when women are equal in numbers equality is automatically achieved. Women *are* in the majority in adult education but the problem of under-development remains the same, as it is men who continue to control the policies and resources and make the definitions, rules and interpretations. Unfortunately there are no complete national figures which show the breakdown of full and part-time staff in adult education by sex (see DES: 1983: Table 5). Nan Whitbread shows that the number of full-time teachers in local education authority adult education has increased nearly threefold from 719 in 1976 to 2037 in 1982. Women's participation has grown by 3% to 40% in the same period. She notes that the Department of Education and Science includes welfare and nursery training centres within these adult education figures. The table below shows where teachers are allocated within the career structures:

Prin & VP	20.4	12.5	28.0	18.3	4.3	13.2
HoD & PL	38.5	11.4	10.3	27.4	6.7	11.4
SL	33.3	3.4	3.9	42.0	6.7	6.3
LII	34.8	32.2	34.9	49.0	30.4	21.4
LI	52.2	40.1	21.3	42.6	51.8	47.1

Note: DES definitions are not consistent 1975-1982

(Whitbread: 1984: 18-21).

During this period women lost ground at senior management level (principal, vice-principal, head of department and principal lecturer). Surprisingly, they have also decreased their share of the lowest grade (Lecturer I), where men have increased sixfold to women's fourfold. However since 1976 women have made considerable progress into middle management grades (Lecturer II and Senior Lecturer). It remains to be seen whether they will be blocked at this level.

Although the Inner London Education Authority (ILEA) employs far more full-time staff than any other local education authority, the position of women should not be dissimilar to the situation in other parts of Britain. At the reorganisation of its adult education service into fewer but larger institutes in January 1980, there were 20 male principals and only 2 female where there had formerly been 7. Reorganisation in education generally appears to result in the reduction in the numbers of senior posts for women (Spender: 1982: 44). At the vice-principal level the proportion was virtually equal – 11 men to 13 women. Not surprisingly, at the bottom end of the scale, Lecturer I and Lecturer II, there were 63 men and 153 women.[3] This situation of where women are placed in the hierarchy is confirmed by the research of Mee and Wiltshire who found that in the local education sector there were 87.3 per cent male organisers and only 12.7 per cent women (nearly 9 men to every woman) – by organisers they mean someone with responsibility for programme planning (1978: 59). The salaries of these senior staff in the Local Education Authorities sector are usually directly related to the number of students which helps to perpetuate inbuilt conservatism.

In the British university adult education departments in 1978/79 there were only 12 women at senior lecturer level and above compared with 193 men.[4] And in the Workers' Educational Association all 3 national officers are men, as are 19 out of 21 district secretaries. It is difficult to find accurate figures on the number of part-time tutors generally (not even the Department of Education and Science collect these figures) but it is assumed that women, as in the general labour market, are in the majority. In Britain only 709,000 men work part-time compared with 3,759,000 women (Department of Employment, *Employment Gazette*: December 1982).[5] In the Inner London Education Authority, for example, in March 1983 women were 59.5 per cent of the hourly paid tutors (4263 compared with 2900 men). But 72 per cent of the tutors working over ten hours per week were women (502 compared with 193 men).[6] In March 1983 the General Secretary of the Association for Adult and Continuing Education (AACE), Lucia Jones, estimated that 80 per cent of all part-time tutors were women as indicated by a survey in Croydon. Even this union is not able to show equality at decision-making levels: only 38.9 per cent of branch secretaries, 28.6 per cent of regional secretaries and 18.5 per cent of national executive members are women (Roy Parker, President: July 1983). These statistics reveal the position and situation of women working and studying in adult education. They are the majority in numbers but the minority in the power structures.

The Department of Education and Science in its collation of statistics sometimes subsumes adult education figures within the further education sector but can also merge them with the youth service. Even our political masters do not seem to see adult education as a service in its own right. Could this be because it is seen as a 'woman's service' and is also marginal in the totality of education provision in Britain: 73 per cent of the national education budget is spent on schools compared with 0.66 per cent in adult education (Bayliss: 1982). Hence it has little political bite in relation to the bigger budgets and power bases of the rest of the education world. It tends to be reactive rather than innovative, and almost apologetic in times of economic cut-backs about its importance and place within continuing education and society in general. There is a tendency to justify adult education and its achievements not in its own right as good, life-enhancing and necessary, but in terms of being the solution to other things – loneliness, lack of social contact, useful, a means to some vaguely defined end. It seems to have lost its early crusading zeal of education being the way to change. It is an instrument to confirm the powers-that-be and to uphold the status quo. The same qualities that are valued or noted in women generally, and specifically in their role within the family such as being passive rather than active, modest, caring, servicing, being able to exist on a shoe-string budget, fragmented and tolerant, can be applied to the adult education service. This is both its potential strength and its existing weakness.

So far we have concentrated on an over-view of where women are in adult education – in fact shown them hidden within the figures and structures. The Case Studies which follow show some of the places where women can be in adult education. Their interest is in their individual and local experience, but their strength is in the way that women have innovated and learned together. Sometimes they have succeeded; sometimes they have faded away as needs or groups have changed. They show the possibilities and exhilarations of co-operation, as well as the problems of trying to work within existing educational ideas and structures. They are signals that adult education has to stop mixing its messages of being open to change and yet in practice preserving the status quo.

Notes

1 In the two years from 1979 the numbers of one-parent families grew from 860,000 to 978,000.
2 See Marthe Sansregret, *The Recognition of Women's Experiential Learning in the United States*: 1983 for a detailed account on research approaches and findings on experiential learning projects. Interestingly it was found in one project on access that the women in the survey had an average of 16 years' home-making experience, but that 40% of them had mended cars, done carpentry or construction work, repaired electrical or plumbing equipment; and that 'the skills identification activity was a positive experience ... improving the self-concept of the participant' (202).
3 Leisha Fullick, Southwark Adult Education Institute in London, has kindly let us see these figures.
4 Thanks to Leni Oglesby, University of Sheffield, for compiling these figures from the *Commonwealth Universities Yearbook* 1980. Since then a woman Professor has been appointed to Glasgow University.
5 A survey that indicates the tendency in the employment pattern in terms of gender, of part-time tutors, was published as long ago as 1970 (NIAE:

Adult Education – Adequacy of Provision: March 1970). In the 1967/68 session 309 part-time tutors out of 552 (a 56% response rate) from seven enquiry areas, answered questionnaires. 85% of the tutors worked in the Local Education Authority sector and only 15% in the Responsible Bodies. Of these 309 tutors nearly 40% had a full-time job in education, 25% worked in business or commerce; 'the balance was made up of housewives' (33%) and people retired from full-time work (3%) (*Adult Education*, vol. 42: 6 March 1970: 172-3). A recent survey estimated that for about 60% of the women part-time staff it was their only paid work; the same situation applied to only 3.5% of the male staff (Islington Adult Education Institute 1984).

6 Statistics Division: The Inner London Education Authority, November 1983.

Part II

Case Studies

Section 1 – Access

1 The Educational Guidance Service for Adults in Northern Ireland
Dorothy Eagleson: additions by the authors

There are now nearly fifty educational guidance services in the British Isles. The Belfast Service was the first of these and, indeed, the first in Europe. Founded in 1967 on the initiative of the Clement Wilson Foundation, funded also by the Gulbenkian Foundation, it functioned under the auspices of the Northern Ireland Council of Social Services (NICSS). It serves the whole of the Province, though most of its clients come from the Greater Belfast area and adjoining districts.

The Educational Guidance Service for Adults (EGSA) is now an independent entity, in association with the NICSS, which acts as Trustee, and is recognised by the Commissioners of Inland Revenue as a Charity.

The Management Committee, members of which are representative of, though not representing, various interests in adult education, is the employing body and determines policy, negotiates funding and approves the appointment of staff. An Honorary Finance Officer looks after the accounts.

The Service received Government funding after its first three years, but this was withdrawn after the then Minister for Education in Northern Ireland, Lord Melchett, decided that the responsibility for such services should lie with the Education and Library Boards. However, the Service continued to function through voluntary donations while clients, referrers and supporters launched a campaign of protest locally, in Great Britain and abroad. This resulted in the setting up, by the Minister, of a

Committee to look into the provision of guidance services in Northern Ireland, and of the interim restoration of funding. After publication of the Jackson Committee's Report in 1979 which recommended that there should be both voluntary and statutory provision (few of the recommendations have been implemented so far), EGSA was guaranteed ongoing funding of 90 per cent, directly from the Department of Education (NI). The other 10 per cent is found through the Service having a consultancy role for a number of organisations, and acting as an agent for Channel 4 and Ulster Television in contributing to and disseminating back-up information for adult education programmes.

The Service stresses its independence of the providers of adult education as being of the first importance. It is perceived by clients and referrers as being impartial, free from pressures and, above all, client-centred. It has very close links with all the providers, statutory and voluntary, formal and informal, and is able to draw their attention to consumer needs; a number of courses in Northern Ireland now exist because of suggestions made by EGSA.

In 1982-3 there were over four hundred queries on a wide range of topics from individuals who telephoned, wrote or visited the office. The staff were also involved in group discussions with, for example, women on housing estates, through attendance at events sponsored by the Council of Continuing Education, such as the Festival of Youth, and at Further Education Colleges' Open Days. Information was given not only on conventional adult education but on courses offered by Leisure Centres, the Sports Council, events sponsored by Museums and the Arts Council and special interest groups, e.g. NIACRO – The Northern Ireland Association for the Care and Rehabilitation of Offenders, the Northern Ireland Association for Mental Health and the Law Centre.

In 1982-3, 174 women and 170 men had a first interview whilst 122 women and 134 men had follow-ups. 39 per cent of the women and 35 per cent of men were under 25 and the remainder over. More women than men (110 to 82) had attained 'O' levels or higher qualifications and substantially more had completed their previous studies (43 to 24). It is interesting that 26 per cent of the women and only 19 per cent of the men had been involved in higher education which may suggest that even with academic qualifications women find it more difficult than men to return to work or study. A list of the present occupations of clients, not broken down by sex, is included. It appears to exclude housewives, who are probably not seen as having an occupation.

PRESENT OCCUPATIONS

Architectural assistant	1	Packer	1
Accountancy trainee	1	Photographical trainee	1
Barman	2	Plasterer	1
Binman	1	Play group organiser	1
Own business	5	Pool attendant	1
Caterer	6	Porter	1
Child care assistant	2	Power worker	1
Civil servant	11	Postman	1
Cleaner	2	Purchasing officer	1
Clerk	20	Receptionist	1
Computer programmer	1	Recreation manager	1
Dental hygienist	1	Researcher	1
Development officer	1	Religious order/clergy	3
Diver	1	Sales manager	1
Electrician	3	Salesman	2
Engineer	1	Secretary	3
Executive	1	Security service	2
Farmer	1	Shop assistant	4
Fireman	1	Social worker	1
Florist	1	Stock controller	1
Gardener	1	Switchboard operator	1
Health visitor	1	Teacher	1
Home help	1	Telephone engineer	1
Housing visitor	1	Technician	2
Industrial conciliator	1	Tool maker	1
Joiner	1	Training instructor	1
Laboratory assistant	1	Typist	4
Leisure centre manager	1	Van driver	1
Librarian	1	Vehicle builder	2
Nurse	5	Voluntary organisation	
Student/pupil nurse	6	helper	4
		Warden	1

(EGSA: 16th Annual Report 1982/3: 11/12)

The age range of the clients is from 19 to over 60, and they come from all social, educational, religious, and political backgrounds, many from outside the Greater Belfast area. Most come through other clients, but about one-third are referred by social workers, psychiatrists, voluntary organisations such as the Marriage

Guidance Council and the Samaritans. Many clients have psychiatric or psychological problems or are physically handicapped and need supportive counselling, and the mental health aspect of the Service's work is important. It may refer for appropriate help clients identified as being 'at risk'. Others have sought information from educational providers and are sent to the Service so that they can find out all about the possibilities open to them and relate them to their abilities, needs and aspirations. Listed below are the types of educational queries dealt with by the Service:

General Education	160
General University/Degree Courses	50
Reading/Spelling Problems	16
Telepohone and Written Queries	400 +
Adult Literacy Queries	300 +

(EGSA: 1982-3: 12)

Where it is difficult to make assessments from interview the Service's psychologist uses psychological tests, mainly of academic potential. A number of the women are widowed, divorced, separated, single parents; some are depressed, coping with difficult domestic and financial circumstances; many, however, are working, or 'ordinary housewives' seeking to develop special interests sometimes so that they can be more effective in voluntary work, or younger women who may be late developers or finding opportunities to consider their future for the first time. The following table (EGSA: 1982-3: 12) indicates that there were 41 potential occupations mentioned by the clients and lists the 9 most popular, social work and teaching being the first choices:

Business management	5
Computing	7
Engineering	5
Nursing	8
Personnel management	5
Social work	20
Secretarial work	5
Teaching	13
Youth work	5

Some are being encouraged by husbands, boyfriends, families, but occasionally the first approach towards adult education is tentative and may be concealed because of the uncertainty of reaction.

A number tend to under-estimate their abilities and aim at courses which may be of too low a level or are otherwise inappropriate; some do not realise that their particular talents or experience could be built on and developed usefully. Younger women include some who have not completed a course started after leaving school, did not have the opportunity to continue their education because of family circumstances, or were not encouraged to do so; some *have* completed a course but wish to update and broaden their qualifications or, sometimes, to change direction completely in the light of the greater awareness, in maturity, of their own needs and abilities, and changing circumstances.

The Service is involved in the adult literacy programme, organising the Referral Service for Northern Ireland, but fewer women than men seek help with reading or spelling problems. (See also Case Study No. 2.) At the end of the educational spectrum are women who are graduates or otherwise qualified and wish to update their qualifications, add to them, or use them differently.

Adult education provision in Northern Ireland is fairly good in and near Belfast, less so elsewhere, especially in rural areas. Once basic qualifications have been obtained, mature students can go to university, polytechnic, colleges of education and colleges of further education, which also offer general certificate of education exams, refresher and introductory courses. The WEA is strong in Northern Ireland, there are extra-mural or continuing education departments in the two universities and the polytechnic, two independent adult colleges, and an increasing amount of development in community education. Provision specifically for women is increasing.

As elsewhere, the heavy unemployment rate in Northern Ireland has resulted not only in numbers of women becoming redundant, but in fewer opportunities for those wishing to return to work, or change direction. The emphasis on continuing education must now often be for personal development, or voluntary work. Despite this, many of EGSA's clients have become nurses, teachers, administrators, social workers: some have taken business studies or computing courses, but there has been little interest in science or technology amongst older women.

The 'New Opportunities for Women' course in the Ulster

Polytechnic has enabled a number of EGSA's clients to take their first steps towards both formal and informal adult education. The opportunity to sample subjects, to learn with other women, to expand horizons, has been much appreciated. One client who took her degree as a mature student is now teaching on the course.

2 Women in Literacy and Adult Basic Education: Barriers to Access
Juliet McCaffery

Several aspects of the developments in Adult Basic Education over the last ten years deserve closer attention. The available evidence suggests that more men than women are taking up opportunities to improve their basic skills. A research project into the progress of literacy students by the National Foundation of Educational Research in 1976 revealed a ratio of 65:35 male and female students (Gorman: June 1981). The number of women decreased in the following three years and dropped as low as 20 per cent (Charnley and Jones: 1978: 12). The most recent information suggests a slightly higher ratio. The National Children's Bureau found that 10 per cent of those born in the week 3-9 March 1958 had literacy problems and a further 5 per cent numeracy problems. More men than women (12:7) reported literacy problems, though difficulties with numeracy were reported equally by men and women. In both cases men were far more likely to attend classes than women. 10 per cent of the men and 5 per cent of the women went to literacy classes; this compares to 10 per cent of the men and only 2.5 per cent of the women going to numeracy classes (National Child Development Study: 1983).

Our experience at the Friends Centre, a Voluntary Adult Education Centre in Brighton, East Sussex, shows a similar pattern. The Centre currently offers three basic education programmes: a full-time Preparatory Training Opportunities Course, a part-time course, both funded by the Manpower Services Commission (MSC) and a Voluntary Literacy Scheme funded by the Local Education Authority as part of the county's literacy provision. This relies heavily on the assistance of voluntary literacy tutors, 90 per cent of whom are women. The Centre also ran a Second Chance/New Horizons general education course from 1978 to 1980 and shorter evening courses in the following two years. An

European Economic Community (EEC) funded two-year project in basic computing and numeracy, with particular reference to women, started in September 1983. The proportion of men to women in 1983 on the three existing courses at the Friends Centre are as follows:

Proportion of Women from 1.1.83 to 31.3.83 (%)			
Full-time	*Part-time*	*Voluntary scheme*	
		Day	*Evening*
Women	18	33	43	18
Men	82	66	57	82

Other centres show a similar pattern, with more women attending daytime classes or part-time courses than evening classes or full-time courses. The table below show the percentage of women students in several schemes from 1.1.83 to 31.3.83:

Beauchamp Lodge Literacy Scheme, London	35
Canning Street Adult Education Centre, Liverpool	37
Hull Local Education Authority	20
Shrewsbury Local Education Authority	33

Very little attention has been given to the lower intake of women although the majority of literacy and basic education tutors are women. Basic education is still a low priority area in adult education in all but the major urban centres. Only 0.1% of the education budget is spent on adult basic education (Wells, Alan: Adult Literacy and Basic Stills Unit (ALBSU) Speech 1983). Resources are stretched to the limit, but even within these limitations women are not receiving their fair share.

There are many reasons why women do not seek help. Basic education cannot be treated in isolation. It is impossible not to correlate this area with women's lack of achievement in other areas of education and view the low numbers of women participants as due to administrative ignorance and lack of interest, reflecting the lack of importance attached to womë's education by both men and women themselves.

The publicity surrounding the literacy campaign of the mid-

1970s created lasting images both of those needing help and the help itself. The BBC programme and the Literacy Unit's publicity posters showed men and women receiving literacy provision, but the image created and reflected in the two key 'On the Move' characters was of capable hard-working men, denied job opportunities and promotion prospects and concealing their inadequacy from their wives and families. Articles in the press emphasised the sensational aspects with headlines, using words like 'victim', 'guilt', 'shame', 'creeping'. A recent article on literacy (*The Times* 2.9.1983), featuring the difficulties of three men, suggests that the image has hardly changed in eight years. Nevertheless the BBC deserves full credit for raising the public level of awareness, and through the use of a referral service, forcing the local authorities to provide tuition.

The publicity reflecting the reasons given by those who sought help perpetuates the dominance of men. Common reasons given by men over the years have been recent unemployment and the subsequent need to find a new job, the possibility or offer of promotion and the consequent fear of being 'found out', the possibility of, or need, for, further training, the desire to help and read to their own children, the loss of face in front of children, a change in family circumstances and an increased need to rely on their own skills or the desire to master skills which previously eluded them. Many of these pressures which are work-oriented reflect the male role of provider and force men to overcome extreme embarrassment and anxiety. They may not apply to women to the same extent. Until recently the main reasons given by women were family oriented: to read to the children, help with school work, write notes to the doctor, school and milkman. Further training, job promotion or even job seeking were less frequently cited until the 1980s when the increase in unemployment and the loss of areas of work traditionally held by women created a keener awareness among women of the need to improve basic skills in order to secure any paid employment.

The loss of these areas of work increases pressure on women to consider retraining, but unemployment creates additional negative effects. There is increased pressure to stay at home. Several tutors have commented on the changed character of daytime classes. Where these existed they were predominantly attended by women, often exclusively so, and acted as support groups for the women involved where the demands of conflicting roles and individual anxieties could be talked through in a supportive environment. A tutor in Calderdale, Yorkshire, has noticed a decrease in women's attendance, corresponding to an increase in men at daytime classes. She believes that the changed character of the groups no longer meets women's needs in the same way.

Women do not generally appear as concerned as men if their difficulties are known by other members of the family. They are less embarrassed at being dependent on others. Dependence is part of the traditional role and a lack of literacy skills is just another form of dependence. The inability to read is not seen as a threat to femininity, but does seem to threaten a man's masculinity. However, women share the feeling that society will under-estimate their ability in other areas in which they are perfectly competent. As a student in Brighton commented, 'Why do they want to know if I can spell if they are employing me to make stockings?'

A change in family circumstances, divorce, widowhood or pregnancy, means dealing with officialdom and bureaucracy. The fear of this, compounded by anxiety over lack of basic skills, creates the pressure to seek help. Many women, like men, view themselves as unable to learn and it is only when society brings sufficient pressure to bear that it becomes impossible to retreat and ignore the problem.

Such a pressing need can outweigh the need for a husband's approval if not his active support. Approval is easily given in theory and negated in practice, particularly if the need is not as apparent to the husband. This is as common for women who seek help with basic education as for women who take up any activity, interest or employment outside the home. Many men will not babysit in the evenings. Many women feel it would be unreasonable to ask their husbands to do so. Most tutors will be familiar with this excuse for missing a daytime class. 'I can't come next week, my husband is on holiday and he likes me at home.' Daytime provision makes it possible to come without a husband's knowledge. Increased male unemployment, with the enormous strains it creates on male self-esteem, may curtail many women's freedom of action and increase difficulties even when daytime provision is available, as a Brighton student found: 'I can't come. My husband thinks I should stay at home with the baby. He won't let me take him to a crêche. He says its my job to look after him, not someone else's.' In addition, an improvement in literacy skills fundamentally affects the balance of power in a relationship and threatens the dominance of the partner who is depended upon.

This cultural pattern of women's lives makes the take-up of

opportunities problematic, but this is further compounded by insufficient attention to the physical pattern of women's lives by many institutions and organisers. Although the lower levels of the Adult Basic Education Service, part-time tutors and local organisers are in the main staffed by women, often on an almost casual labour basis, the higher grades and the administration are, as elsewhere in education, dominated by men who decide the pattern of provision and the times and locations of classes. The needs and demands of the institution have to be met, budgets have to be adhered to and the daily rhythm of women's lives revolving around the domestic responsibilities of home, husband and children are frequently not understood or regarded as an inconvenience, not sufficiently important to accommodate. Many schemes like the Friends Centre have no childcare provision compatible with the timing of basic education classes and courses. Moreover childcare is expensive. The regulations, quite rightly, are strict. Budgets are increasingly restricted. Space, as in the case of the Friends Centre, is limited. A principal or organiser has to be totally committed in order to allocate precious resources to childcare provision. Yet experience shows that when there is carefully timed and placed provision, supported by childcare facilities, women respond. The only courses at the Friends Centre to have a majority of women students were the daytime, crêche-supported, New Horizons courses sponsored by the Adult Literacy Unit with 100 per cent women the first year and 80 per cent the second. Centres and institutions with good childcare facilities show a similar response. For example, in Liverpool, particularly, the Parent/School Partnership at Paddington School, Mount Vernon Road and the 'Second Step for Women' run by Norfolk Local Education Authority sponsored by ALBSU in 1982-3 have been tremendously successful in attracting women. Centres with good facilities and an awareness of women's lives, like Peckham Bookplace in South London, have a consistently higher percentage of women compared to the national average.

The use of individual voluntary tutors providing tuition in their own home, or the student's home, provides a flexibility not afforded by the increasing tendency towards centre-based tuition. At the Beauchamp Lodge Centre, London, a spot check in May 1983 showed that 16 out of the 26 women in a total enrolment of 96 had home tuition. The move towards centre-based tuition, now undertaken by two-thirds of the literacy schemes for sound educational reasons, may be unconsciously reducing flexibility for women. Yet home does not provide an ideal learning environment as learning competes with domestic demands. As a Brighton tutor pointed out:

> 'I find it very difficult to teach her. The baby constantly demands attention, or the neighbour calls, or she has to check on the cooking. If I go in the evening when the baby is in bed, we have to use the kitchen. It is very difficult for her to concentrate at home.'

Literacy materials are yet another area where insufficient attention has been given to the needs of women. At the start of the campaign there was little material suitable for either men or women. This lack of material provided one major impetus for the rapid development of student-written material, both more interesting and more suitable for adults than commercial reading schemes. As there were more male students, so more writing of interest to men was published. Although there is some excellent writing by women on a variety of subjects now available, men remain dominant in this area. Two out of eight authors of 'Brighton Books' (Macmillan, 1978), and three individual authors so far published by the Gatehouse Project in Manchester are women, though the last few years have seen an increase in the number of collections of writing written and produced by women (*Every Birth It Comes Different*, Centreprise 1980; *I Want to Write it Down*, Peckham 1980). Fewer community writers are women (examples include, Noakes, Daisy: *A Town Beehive* 1975 and *A Faded Rainbow*: Queen's Spark Pubs., Brighton 1977). In some areas there has been active hostility to the use of specifically female writing. An informal duplicated booklet on childbirth and pregnancy published by a literacy scheme in Kent in 1978 received unwelcome attention from the Authority which deemed such subjects unsuitable for literacy classes.[1] While many working-class people would deny that their lives or experiences were of sufficient value to be recorded in print, women find it harder to overcome the double barrier of both class and sex. A riveting account of life during the war starts: 'My life during the last war was not very exciting. . . .' (Gimbly, Rita, *My War Experiences*: Brighton Writing, 1976).

A group who are equally disadvantaged are women who have sufficient reading and writing skills to 'get by' but who left school at the statutory leaving age to go into unskilled work. The lack of educational facilities in this country enabling such people to move into adult or further education poses a particular problem. Similarly there are few opportunities for those whose basic skills have improved, but whose general education is lacking. Second chance 'New Horizon' courses are particularly attractive to this group. As well as improving writing and communication skills the courses serve the same purpose as the more advanced 'New Opportunities for Women' in providing women with the confidence to move back into the world outside home. Courses run in Brighton, Southampton, London and Liverpool, as well as elsewhere, have been extraordinarily successful in attracting women without any school-leaving qualifications, and many students say later that the experience changed their lives: 'Don't come round Tuesday, I'm starting a job. It's only temporary, but I'd never have done it if I hadn't been on "New Horizons".' (McCaffery, Juliet M.A. Dissertation: University of Sussex 1983.)

Tutors are continually amazed at the impact these courses have on the participants, yet they are the hardest to finance. The inability to write clearly and a general lack of confidence do not have the same emotional appeal as the inability to read. The courses are expensive to run, as they are normally two days a week and require crèche/playgroup provision. Our experience at Brighton has shown that most women are quite unable to afford realistic fees. Yet far more of these courses are needed if women are to compete with their male counterparts in the employment market.

Basic education courses run by the Manpower Services Commission (MSC) for adults over 19 years of age are perhaps the least flexible of all basic education provision and effectively discriminate against women. Preparatory courses, preparing trainees in the basic skills enabling them to proceed to further training or employment are full-time, five days a week, from 9.00 a.m. to 5.00 p.m. with no provision for childcare even though many women will eventually take up part-time employment. The part-time course at the Friends Centre is a pilot project and the table on p. 63 shows its advantage for women students. Yet this course, unlike the full-time preparatory course, does not entitle a trainee to a training or a travelling allowance. Although the course is free, there can be hidden costs for women. One woman unable to maintain childcare and travel costs of £11.90 per week for three mornings finally left the course.

Government retraining programmes effectively discriminate against women. 31 per cent of all Training Opportunity Scheme (TOPs) trainees, including those in non-basic courses, are women. This is well below the percentage of women (40 per cent) in the labour market. All these courses are full-time. Skill Centres frequently start at 8.00 a.m. Even traditionally female courses such as hairdressing do not take school time into account. A trainee on the part-time course in Brighton had to forgo a place at the technical college as she was unable to manage such a long day, yet she desperately needed to acquire a trade (McCaffery, Juliet and Rhode, Ursula: *Study and Work*: AUBSU: 1982).

There is some evidence that the Manpower Services Commission (MSC) is aware of the problem. 'A Strategy for Adult Training' (MSC: 1982) suggests possible co-operation with local authorities for childcare provision and suggests that more flexibility is needed, but £500,000 spent in 1981-2 on special training for women does not indicate a major commitment despite the setting up of a few pilot projects like the one at the Deptford Skills Centre (see Case Study No. 10).

Thus despite the growth in adult basic education over the last few years there have been few structural attempts to recruit women in the same numbers as men. It has been left to individual centres and institutions to provide isolated examples of appropriate, flexible provision. The response to these shows that when there is minimal conflict with traditional roles women will respond. One woman echoed many when she said, 'It changed my life.'

Unfortunately many women's lives are not being changed, as they are unable to take advantage of provision in their area. There has been very little enquiry into the depressing and isolating effects of illiteracy on women. Women are not seen to be held back in the same way as men. Yet a lack of competence in basic skills isolates in the same way as a high-rise apartment or an outlying housing estate. It adversely affects women's whole lives.

Note

1 Note also the Scottish Health Education's Council's banning of the 'Well Women' pamphlet to accompany a TV series 1982-3.

3 Education of Asian Women
Saroj Seth

It is fair to say that the need for education, and its values and significance in enabling a person to face the harsh realities of life are recognised by Asian people to a greater extent than their

Western counterparts. This is due to a variety of reasons, the most important being the economic one, that is to secure better employment through gaining educational qualifications. As many Asian parents, especially mothers, have missed out on their own education in their homelands they are most anxious about their children's, especially daughters', educational achievements.

Many reports have been published over the years by various organisations about the under-achievement of Asian children, especially girls, in schools. Asian girls in particular should be encouraged by their parents to participate fully in all the various school activities, e.g. camping, school trips, language exchanges, dramatic productions, etc., so that they grow up feeling that they are part of the school community. This does not mean that they should, or would, give up their traditional way of life. If a girl is considered by her teachers as good enough for higher education, she should be given every encouragement by her parents to acquire this. In many ways the schools have not been able to utilise fully the special gifts and talents of Asian children, e.g. in science and mathematics. This is particularly true of Asian girls who get very little support from their school careers officers for higher education or in terms of career guidance. The cautious attitudes of the schools' career officers is because they make undue allowance for the girl's home background. Parents and authorities could both help in providing the girl with facilities for continuing her education by, for example, giving priority to her attending the local university and continuing to live at home with her parents. The local education authorities should be made aware of the fact that Asian women students, in particular, should be given as much guidance and facilities as possible to obtain qualifications so that they can participate and contribute positively to a multi-racial society such as Britain. Primary and secondary school teaching is a career thought to be most suitable for Asian girls, as this would bring about greater integration, harmony and closer co-operation between Asian parents and education authorities in areas of high immigrant population. These locally trained Asian women teachers would be able to share their talents and cultural backgrounds with those of the host community, because of their understanding of both cultures. In turn, their pupils, both Asian and indigenous, would grow up with more tolerance and consideration of each other.

As more emphasis is placed upon teaching English, one must also not forget the need to maintain the children's mother tongues and their bilingual background. Mother-tongue proficiency and the bilingual background confers special benefits on the children and is definitely not a handicap to learning English as is often made out. The child is able to learn correct grammatical English and also finds it easier to cope with another language at the 'O' or 'A' level stage. There is the additional advantage of identifying oneself with one's community as there is an emotional need for this. I hope more and more local education authorities will provide facilities for bilingual education in schools. Alongside this a more broad-based school curriculum should be developed including the study of Asian history, geography, art and music. Revised topic books will not only give Asian children the chance to learn about their 'roots' but also help the indigenous children by dispelling some of the myths and outdated information which are still circulating in textbooks and libraries.

In this country Asian women are characterised as being homebound. This idea cannot be reconciled when one sees leaders such as the late Mrs Gandhi of India and Mrs Banderanaike of Sri Lanka. These women are hardly characteristic of homebound Asian women. It is true, however, that most of these remarkable women came from a narrow band of the upper class which is no different from English and French women who have been leaders in their society.

Having dealt with several women's groups in Leicester, it is, however, abundantly clear to me that Asian women in Britain have a double disadvantage. Firstly, having left their homes either in the subcontinent or in East Africa many are living in difficult conditions and coping with alien surroundings with little or no knowledge of the English language or culture. A recent survey based on a sample of Asian women in Britain found that 77 per cent of Pakistani women knew very little or no English, whilst the corresponding percentage for East African Asian women was 40 per cent. This creates a barrier for these women when having to deal with the prolems of everyday life such as shopping, applying for pensions, social security, visiting schools, hospitals and clinics, etc. This problem is very serious for the first generation of Asian women. Six- or seven-year-old children are often used by their mothers as interpreters, thus putting tremendous strains on them and keeping the women in a dependent position both within and outside the home. It is not easy to step into a highly industrialised, progressive, fast and developed city in Britain, having come from a rural background in the subcontinent. In most cases the women have been forced to leave their homes to follow their husbands.

Secondly, the Asian women, classified as black women when they work outside the home, do so for the lowest wages in the hardest and most difficult conditions. They are subjected to discrimination and pettiness of all kinds that is not shown to their western counterparts. In the present harsh economic climate in this country these women have no choice but to agree to these unacceptable terms of employment and conditions of service for fear of being without work. The most vociferous ones are not easily accepted and are somehow or other either sacked or not promoted.

Asian women feel responsible as the guardians and defenders of the traditions of their own forefathers, whilst at the same time they are going through a cultural shock adapting to life in an alien city. As mothers they feel their traditional role is to transmit the language, customs and religion of their country to their children. Children attend schools where the values, language and the traditions of the host country are the only ones taught. This causes all kinds of anxieties for the mothers who have a very significant role to play in moulding lives, their daughters' especially.

There are numerous differences of opinion about the changes taking place in the position of Asian women in the United Kingdom. Some people regard these changes as profound, and are of the opinion that the increasing participation by women in public life or elsewhere has given them more status. Others maintain that the position of women has changed very little in Indian society which is very male-orientated. The position of women is not the same amongst the Hindus and Muslims, in different parts of the country and most particularly in the different social strata. The segregation of women is of course closely associated with certain religious beliefs and practices. In general segregation is practised to a greater extent among Muslims than among Hindus. This seems to be more an aspect of the Islamic cultural tradition than of Islamic religious beliefs.

From my experience of dealing with Asian women in Leicester, the majority of women that go out to work are mostly from the Hindu and Sikh communities. Muslim women tend to stay at home and look after the families. With much persuasion and trust and years of hard work, I have managed to get Muslim women out of their homes to come to Ladies-only classes and activities at school. Regular Ladies-only social and cultural evenings, outings, swimming and keep-fit activities are organised which are very popular with Muslim women as they have no other source of entertainment, because of their rigid religious beliefs. More and more Bangladeshi women have started coming to the English classes, yet there is a lot of education required to be transmitted to this special group of women.

There are vast class and educational differences among the Asian women in Britain. One finds that the more affluent and educated women from the middle classes have accepted and adapted themselves well within this society. They enjoy the same social norms and activities as their English counterparts, whereas the ordinary housewife, mother of a large family with language problems, finds it extremely difficult to cope with life. She is still clinging to the trappings of her traditions and customs in which she finds comfort and security. At the same time this special category of women still retains a certain pride and independence which is a contradiction and quite remarkable when one sees the difficulties they face.

As much as I believe in integration, there are certain areas where separatism or positive discrimination will be more beneficial in relation to Asian women. For instance the whole question of the special needs of Asian women in terms of language classes, organised activities, sheltered accommodation for battered Asian wives, forces us to look and move towards separatism rather than integration. These facts cannot be ignored as one has to bear in mind these women's special religious, social, cultural and dietary requirements. There are certain areas concerning Asian women where total integration will not be feasible or acceptable.

Note

See also Westwood, Sallie & Hoffman, Dallah: 1979, *Asian Women: Education and Social Change*, University of Leicester, School of Education.

Saroj Seth writes about herself: I have been a qualified teacher for twenty-three years, sixteen of them in Britain. I am now the team leader of a bilingual teaching scheme in Leicester. My duties are to set up bilingual teaching schemes in schools in Leicester and provide a support service for my team. I am a Justice of the Peace and also the Chairperson of 'The Roof Group' which provides sheltered accommodation for battered Asian women. I am on the Management Committee of Leicester Council for Community Relations and Treasurer of 'Shanti House' which will provide sheltered accommodation for elderly Asians. I was the founding member and Chairperson of Leicester Asian Ladies Circle, and also past Secretary and an executive member of the United Kingdom Asian Women's

Conference (UKAWC). I belong to the Police Liaison Committee. I helped to set up the Home Tuition scheme for teaching English to Asian women. All my spare time is taken up with matters of race and community relations as I believe in total equality of mankind regardless of colour, caste or creed.

Section 2 – Courses

4 Breakaway: A Discussion Group for Women
Sally Griffiths, Edinburgh University Settlement

Aims
- to offer women alternative provision, with an educational perspective, to the traditional activities which operate in the community centre, such as keep-fit and mother and toddler groups.
- to make this provision at a time and place convenient to women, with content which is relevant to their lives and allows them to draw on their own experience.
- to give women the opportunity to plan their own programme of discussions.

When and where?
Thursdays, 10.00 a.m. to 12.00 noon in Fisherrow Community Centre, Musselburgh, Scotland.

Co-ordinators
Sally Griffiths, Adult Education Organiser, Edinburgh University Settlement
Pat Brechin, Community Worker, East Edinburgh Community Education Department.

To launch a women's discussion group in November 1981, we offered a programme of five discussion topics:

- Being a housewife
- Consumer affairs

- Mental health
- Local Government
- The media and advertising

While we aimed to encourage women to plan their own series of discussions, we felt that since they had no experience of this type of activity, we could not expect them to say what they wanted without first giving them a taste of what was possible; to continue the food analogy, how can people order what they want to eat if they don't know the language of the menu? We were clear from the outset that we were not attempting to set up a feminist, consciousness-raising group. Our aim was to create an awareness of women's roles in society by exploring topics and issues from a woman's point of view. Publicity stressed the chance to get away from the house and children for a few hours. The most effective publicity we had was front-page coverage in the local paper.

From past experience, we recognised that a crèche would be essential to the success of the discussion group. Pat obtained money from the community education's so-called 'disadvantaged groups budget' to pay a crèche worker and the occasional guest speaker. Official guidelines put young mothers in the category for funding but we successfully had the term extended to include all women at home.

Four women attended the first session along with ourselves. By the end of the pilot there were nine women who were enthusiastic to continue meeting. Ages ranged from the early twenties to late thirties. As group co-ordinators, we took note of the issues which emerged during the six weeks, but were only touched on briefly. We presented this list back to the group who selected some of the topics for future discussions, rejected others and made further suggestions themselves. In this way we arrived at a ten-week programme which included:

- Human relations
- Children's books
- *The War Game*
- Romantic fiction
- Women's sexuality
- Breast education
- Women in other cultures
- Self-help in the community

By using this same method of representing issues to the group, the women planned a further programme:

- Ageing
- Abortion
- Loving and hating
- Parents and children
- Reading *What Society does to Girls* (Nicholson, Joyce: 1977/80: Virago

Over this period, several more women joined the group, with an average of nine or ten attending weekly.

When the group had been meeting for almost a year, they actively recruited seven new members. It became evident that it would be difficult to integrate this number of new members, especially since the newcomers wanted to go over ground already covered by the original members. Everyone decided it would be fairer to allow the original group to meet without the intrusion of new people joining, while the newcomers would form the nucleus of a second women's discussion group, which would seek to attract other women. Both groups meet at the same time and we employ two crèche supervisors who are assisted by one or two teenagers on a Manpower Services Commission (MSC) Youth Opportunities Scheme (YOP). The second group has grown to more than twelve in number and is co-ordinated by Pat, while I continue with the original group.

When Pat and I set out, we had little experience of presenting topics, providing stimulus for discussion or of co-ordinating discussion groups. We developed methods of working as we went along. We were worried at first about the amount of information we would be expected to find, but soon discovered that the women themselves had a lot to contribute simply from their own experience. A good way of getting people talking is to use written extracts; newspaper articles and magazines, poetry and literature. I give a copy to everyone in the group and read the piece aloud. It is also helpful to be ready with a series of questions which move people from talking about the content of the extract to relating what they have read to their own lives. However, the advantage of using a written extract to stimulate discussion is that it gives the group something to focus on and allows people to speak without feeling that they have to talk about themselves. We use this method more than any other, and occasionally we use video. When the women want to acquire more information about issues, such as the Third World or Women's Aid (an organisation that helps battered women through local centres), we invite people along with specialist knowledge.

Our experience has also convinced us of the need to have a group co-ordinator; someone to direct discussions and to respond to shifts in topic, to encourage those who are reticent and dissuade those who are inclined to dominate.

Pat and I have gained much from our experience and from mutual encouragement and support, so that when a second group formed, we felt confident about taking a group each. But what have the women gained from their involvement? Here are some of the comments:

> 'As women we have something in common.'
> 'There is nobody here to tell you what to do or say.'
> 'It's a relaxed atmosphere and enjoyable.'
> 'It's not competitive, you're treated as an equal and you're in on the planning of programmes.'
> 'It stretches your mind.'
> 'It's a change from talking to and about children.'
> 'There is no teacher/pupil split; your opinion is worth something.'

The women have gained in confidence and become more aware of their potential. One woman is going to college. A few are becoming more active in the community, volunteering to work with Women's Aid or taking an interest in the local unemployed workers' centre. We believe in the importance and completeness of the discussion group itself, because it helps women to become stronger within themselves.

5 Sandwich Course for Part-time Tutors of Dress or Embroidery at Loughborough College of Art and Design
Hilary Tinley and Sue Walker

Both Hilary Tinley and Sue Walker are in their mid-thirties and were formally educated at grammar schools; they both attended the above course from April 1981 to March 1982.

Hilary Tinley trained in agriculture and spent twelve years in agricultural administration, mainly in Central London. She made the decision to change to embroidery gradually over the two years prior to starting the course, intending eventually to work full-time at home. The course complemented her study for the City and Guilds Embroidery Certificate and enhanced her earning power from practical work with the opportunity to teach on a part-time basis.

Sue Walker had a fourteen-year career in nursing, is married to an anaesthetist and lives in the West Country. She has wanted for several years to take some course in art or crafts and the opportunity to avail herself of this particular course came at an opportune moment, fitting in with domestic arrangements. The decision was made rather rapidly and it has been only in the following year that she has taken time to reflect on the effect of the course in relation to domestic commitment and further exploration in the field of textiles and design.

The students

All the 25 students were female, between the ages of 21 and 69 years, with the majority falling into the 30-50 age group. Numerous reasons prompted students to take the course, e.g. personal, domestic – failed or problematic marriage – or a desire for individual development outside the family, qualifications as part of a career plan, change of direction, a complement to previous qualifications or pure self-interest.

The very nature of the course arrangement meant that students had to be split into two groups, alternating with each other during term time in three-week blocks at college and home; thus they were destined only to meet twice during the year. This and the labelling of the groups as 'A' and 'B' seemed to create illogical animosity and aggression, perhaps illustrated by an 'A' group student's remark – 'the Beastly "B"s'.

Domestic influence

Each group comprised a number of resident and non-resident members, that is, some resided in a college hostel, some lived locally and others lodged elsewhere.

Those outside the college hostel did seem to feel that they missed out in terms of emotional support, decision-making and the 'out-of-hours' tutorials which sometimes took place at the hostel.

Residential students, in their turn, suffered certain disadvantages, perhaps being unused to hostel life, close proximity to strangers for three-week periods and the constant upheaval of moving backwards and forwards from home to hostel. This did cause physical and emotional strain which local-based students were largely spared. However, in terms of project work at home, there was a greater opportunity for self-motivation and a taste of co-ordinating home life and creative demands remote from tutor support.

The work

Preliminary interviews provided an opportunity both for the selection of students and an exchange of information between students and tutors. Students were given some ideas of the requirements of the course, which in general proved inadequate, probably because, for whatever reason, students only took in a fraction of the information available and were unable to assess the implications in relation to their own lifestyle. The unique nature of the course and the lack of recent experience of formal learning of the majority of the students were also contributary.

Time was divided between academic study with the University of Nottingham and creative training at the College of Art, with a further division in the latter between design and craft subject. This division in itself was an extra strain in that no student was skilled in all three areas and it required some degree of self-discipline to attempt the more difficult ones.

The academic study of adult education provided a particular challenge as this course aimed to attain university standard certification from students with a wide range of previous academic attainment. Similar pressures arose in the areas of design and craft in an effort to gain an overall high standard of work from students of very mixed ability and experience.

Both tutors and students were painfully aware of the short space of time together (only nineteen weeks at college in the year); thus during the blocks there were regular evening sessions built into the programme and most students felt it imperative to work late on free evenings to keep up the pace of work expected.

Most students, periodically, had feelings of panic, when faced with researching and writing academic projects, learning new skills and being creative all at once, and found themselves floundering in a state of indecision. However, tutors were aware of this and came to the rescue promptly so as not to waste precious time.

Between the students the pressure showed in the conflict of group co-operation and support with the need to maintain one's own level of achievement and individual progress almost at the expense of the others. In theory the course was not competitive, each student having her own objectives for the course. However, there seemed to be an underlying sense of competition which affected some more than others, plus an anxiety that one's own ideas might be used by others.

Most students displayed their particular anxieties indirectly which ranged from petty niggling over domestic arrangements in hostel or studio, exaggerated joviality or an apparently casual approach, to open panic, emotional outbursts and unprovoked attacks on other students. For the most part the group managed to provide support where necessary and potential disasters were avoided, though sometimes a tense atmosphere pervaded.

Continued effort during the first half-year was largely a matter of faith on the part of the students, encouraged strongly by the tutors, as progress seemed an uphill struggle with minimum result. During the final term, however, everything began to fall into place and the final aims were within reach; these being a public exhibition of craft work for assessment and a selection of the completed written work fit to be presented for external assessment. The sense of anti-climax and exhaustion was evident by the final day and everyone had to face the reality of taking up where they had left off, some with more relish than others, and adapting their new skills to their home situation.

Afterwards

There was now the prospect of having to complete a 5,000-word-long study and a teaching assessment for the university during the next year. Motivation towards these, particularly the long study, which would require a good deal of time and research, was often lacking, as the more immediate demands of family or the need to make a living took precedence and even made college work seem increasingly irrelevant. Since the end of the course, for the most part, contact between students has been lost, so little can be said as to how they all feel about the course a year on.

Conclusion

There were a lot of tensions and anxieties during the year and the unique nature of the course probably exaggerated these, with the sandwich arrangement causing a split in the group, the dual certification pulling students in two directions and the shortness of the course proper, which served only to whet the appetite for more.

However, the high expectations of the tutors certainly dragged out of every student resources hitherto untapped and all were surprised by their achievements in that year, making all the effort and agony worthwhile.

6 Women in Public Life – Leadership Training
Gill Boden, Tutor, Department of Extra-Mural Studies, University College, Cardiff

In 1980, with the help of a grant from the Equal Opportunities Commission (EOC), a small group from the Wales Women's Rights Committee designed a course to help women to enter public life.

We had looked at political parties, trade union organisations and a huge range of voluntary bodies and though there was no shortage of women (in some cases, churches for example, organisations were dominated by women) what we found was that women were not in decision-making positions; in other words, to rearrange the wording of a well-known badge we were making tea not policy! We had also looked at the characteristics of those women who *were* successful in public life. We had been told that women 'didn't want the responsibility', 'wouldn't put themselves forward'. The Welsh Office, for example, responsible for finding lay-people to sit on the Arts Council, area health boards, consumer protection bodies and the like, was apt to enquire plaintively where on earth they could find the women prepared and qualified for such public service.

We interviewed twenty local women from different areas of public life – a Member of the European Parliament, a Justice of the Peace (JP), a mayor, local councillors, trade union officials, church workers and women who managed to combine several of these roles. There were some common factors – most of the women had an early start in their chosen field often because of enthusiastic parents so that they were able to amass experience before the child-rearing years (all the women except one were mothers). Their confidence was also helped later on by supportive families (all the women were or had been married).

We became convinced that more women would want to offer their services to some aspect of public life, usually unpaid but not always, if

(a) they had more knowledge of the organisations involved, and
(b) they had the skills to cope with and be critical of expectations surrounding female participation in affairs outside the home.

So we tried to design a course which would fulfil these two objectives.

In practice, this resulted in a course consisting of seven workshops of one or two days each. These were held at weekends to cater for students employed outside the home, but breaks were timetabled in the sequence so that people would not be working non-stop from the start to the finish of the course. It lasted about three months altogether.

We dismissed evenings from the beginning as that would have meant a very long course lacking in the intensity that a whole-day workshop can bring. The seven workshops were called:

1 Starting the Course
2 Perceptions, Attitudes, Motivations and Planning
3 Assertiveness Training
4 Groups and Organisations
5 Organisations specific to Public Life
6 Public Relations and Interacting with the Media
7 Feedback and Critique of the Course

Between the sixth and seventh workshop each student gained some practical experience by working for a short period of about forty hours in some area of public life and produced a report of her internship. These reports made fascinating reading – one student was lucky enough to spend a week at Westminster with Jo Richardson, a Member of Parliament.

We had the difficult task of selection before the course began, as we were over-subscribed. We interviewed each student individually and selected on the basis of predicting who would benefit most from the course – on the basis of a record of involvement in public life or a clear commitment. We also aimed at a 'balanced' intake in terms of age, class and interest.

The group that emerged was fairly well spread in terms of age (with a range of 29 to 59 years). There was a definite bias toward middle-class women, but with a good spread of interest. Two women were aiming to be JPs (one already was one), two women were standing for election for local councils, one was physically handicapped and becoming more and more involved in voluntary work with other handicapped people. Several women were committed feminists, three very active in Women's Aid and in particular in the Peace Movement. We also had students involved in the movement for the Welsh language, the church, and in their trade union.

We had enormous problems in condensing the course into what turned out to be about twelve days. (Another reason of course for not making the course any longer was that the sort of women it attracted were busy people.)

Our second major problem was pedagogical; we wanted after all to encourage a positive attitude towards leadership – but not an uncritical one – we wanted to supply a model within the course team that was authoritative not authoritarian, democratic and effective without being hierarchical, and all the time conscious of a feminist framework – and we wanted our teaching to reflect this. We also wanted the students to have autonomy within the course – all this bounded by the very strict time constraints we had set ourselves.

This gave rise to some tension and it was a difficult, even painful, course to be involved in. It had forced us to take a long hard look at the sometimes, on my part at least, rather woolly notions we held about leadership, power and the women's movement. We had to face up to the rather unpalatable fact that in a publicly funded extra-mural course, some of our students might not be, and in the event were not, feminists; that we might be training women to work for organisations, for example political parties, that as individual members of the course team we had strong reservations about; and we had to stick firmly to our conviction that it was a good thing to train women as women to enter fields dominated by men, as that in itself will hasten the progress of change.

I think we could safely claim to have *extended* the students' views of leadership but not necessarily always in the same direction! The biggest change I detected was a far more positive attitude towards feminism from the students who had been wary of the fact that this was a women's course. I am convinced that this was far more a result of the enthusiasm and commitment of the tutors than any overt statement or information given.

I would go further and guess that for those students, changes in their attitude towards power and leadership will be, in the long term, a result of their changing attitude towards feminism.

In spite of, and perhaps because of, all this, I believe it was a very successful course. The students (fourteen of them) were enthusiastic and for many of them it was as 'life-changing' an experience as it was for us. Students were highly motivated – there was no drop out.

We have not yet repeated the course – it was fairly exhausting to run – but we are still working on a handbook to encourage other groups of women to run similar courses. We hope they will.

Section 3 – Extending the Subject

7 Working with Childminders
Sue Owen

Sue Owen has worked in the pre-school field since 1968 and is currently Information Officer to the National Childminding Association. She is also working on a study of the work process of childminding and minders' attitudes to their work, by means of extended interviews with a cross-section of childminders.

Childminding is the largest form of full day care for pre-school children in the country. The figures can be unreliable, but there are around 45,000 women who are registered to take other people's children into their own homes for all or part of the day. There is also a large number of women who do the job without registering; strictly this is illegal but, for obvious reasons, social services departments rarely have the resources or inclination to hunt down offenders. A much more positive response to the legislation[1] is to use it as a vehicle for bringing support, advice and training to the thousands of women who do this immensely important work, and more and more local authorities are taking this attitude. It is still true that the importance of the work is often not recognised and this can give rise to a very destructive clash of opinions. You frequently hear childminders described in terms such as 'just mums', 'neighbours doing what they know best', 'women who can't or won't leave the house', and, despite years of effort to the contrary, childminding still has a very low status. On the simplest level this is because of the twin and mutually reinforcing facts that it attracts very low rates of pay and that it is women's work, based in the home: something to be done alongside the housework.

However, most people who work with childminders soon learn to appreciate the complexity of the occupation. Childminders all do the job entirely differently, bringing different knowledge and skills to bear and needing different sorts of support and advice. The complexities of childminding arise in some part from the fact that it is a public service which is conducted very privately, in the home. Training is a vital but contentious subject. In fact it causes so much misunderstanding that now it is rarely called training at all, but is usually subsumed under the term 'support', or twinned with it in 'training and support services'. Take, for instance, Joyce Beckwith's explanation in her report on training and support seminars held all over the country during 1981-2:

> when the term 'training and support' is used this implies that these two activities are inextricably intertwined and that training is only one aspect of the total support system, and, secondly, the word 'childminding' is used rather than 'childminders' because we are talking about a care relationship that involves *all* partners in the arrangement, with parent, childminders and local authority workers having a degree of responsibility and 'sharing' the care, often with other members of the wider family and community. So, we are not merely talking about the training of childminders. To do so would neglect the dynamic, interacting relationship between them. (Beckwith: 1982)

One obvious problem connected with training concerns the nature of childminders and the job they do. Most are women with children of their own and many have successfully brought up large families and taken care of other people's children for many years; the last thing they want is to be told how to look after children. This doesn't necessarily mean that they are resistant to learning. All over the country thousands of childminders are attending and requesting courses, but, as Joyce Beckwith's survey showed, childminders overwhelmingly favour courses in which knowledge is pooled rather than handed down by 'teacher'. Formal teaching methods may seem attractive and easier, especially for women with little experience of group discussion but this is, in the long run, unsatisfying and unsuccessful.

This goes some way towards explaining the use of the term 'support'. It is far less threatening than the notion of training and it more accurately describes the situation of childminders who are, for the most part, already doing a good job but need far more recognition and better facilities; among which will be the opportunity to learn extra skills.

A wide range of support services have developed since local authorities and voluntary organisations began to take an interest in childminders in the early 1970s: toy libraries, drop-in centres, combining a playgroup for the children with an informal meeting place for minders, loan schemes of large equipment such as double pushchairs, stair-gates and fireguards, and courses covering everything from basic first aid to tax and social security. Parallel with services offered *to* minders has been the growth of the childminders' own organisations: local associations acting as support for their own members and putting pressure on outsiders such as the press, politicians and social workers. Most of the groups now add a national perspective by affiliating to the National Childminding Association which has been in existence since 1977.

People within childminding tend to see all such developments as part of the same continuum: you can learn and change as much by running a playgroup or organising a local campaign for National Childminding Week as you can from attending a series of lectures on child development, and this attitude has been utilised very successfully by some people involved in the training of child-minders. In 1977 I helped to set up the first training course for childminders in Manchester. It was one of the last developments in a project, funded by the Save the Children Fund, which had been running for over two years and which had built on earlier work by Julia McGawley of the Childminding Research Unit. The project had been running a whole series of support services for child-minders but had avoided the subject of formal training on the grounds that we had our work cut out for us organising the informal discussions (evening meetings/drop-ins, etc.) which were, in any case, likely to be more successful. However, training was much talked of at the time and, eventually, we decided to go ahead and run 'a course'. A core group of project 'regulars' signed up for the course which was held at the project's base, where there was a familiar crèche for the children, but it was organised in conjunction with a local college of Further Education which specialised in nursery nurse training.[2]

The course ran every Thursday morning for six weeks and covered obvious topics such as registration and the law, food, first aid, play, etc. but, because childminding is a field in which practice is of more immediate value than theory, we made sure to bring in those people whose jobs brought them into daily contact with minders: social workers involved in registration, health visitors, nursery school teachers, fire ofiicers, etc. The aim, to re-quote Joyce Beckwith, was to involve all the partners to the 'care relationship'. Some of them may have thought they were coming to teach childminders but we knew better![3]

In fact, in this, and in a second course which followed it, the minders were models of politeness whilst still managing to convey that they had a professional stake in the whole process, and opinions, born of experience, about the ways in which childmind-ing should be regulated and supported. The discussions were wide-ranging and fruitful. Perhaps we had become too insular a group: everyone benefited from being brought face to face with other people's ideas, methods and constraints on a regular basis rather than through isolated, one-off seminars. The course was special, more intensive than the regular discussions, even those which had, similarly, featured outside speakers. Nevertheless, the long tradi-tion of informal discussion groups did affect the courses very strongly. The minders and project staff knew each other very well and felt on home ground: they were more willing to talk and argue than minders who attended later college-based courses, and they were already used to talking together and sharing experiences and beliefs. This issue is highlighted by the course run for childminders in Brixton in 1974 by the National Elfrida Rathbone Society:

> The women were still and formal initially. For all of them this was the first time they'd found themselves in such a situation. They had no idea of what to expect and consequently were nervous and unsure.

and the playgroup too. . .

> was very quiet. Almost unnaturally so. The children were well-behaved but unresponsive. There was little curiosity about play materials. Not much talking or crying. (National Elfrida Rathbone Society, *Changing Childminders*: 1976: 4)

The course continued for four full days a week for five weeks, so the situation quickly changed but, on assessing the impact of the course six months later, Brian Jackson, the author, concluded that nothing in the minders' practice had changed. One reason which he gives seems particularly pertinent:

> Again and again the minders tried to keep in touch with each other after the course. But the huge distances of a big city, the lack of private transport, and the everyday fact of toddlers and babies to be

cared for, were too much. If a change in cultural attitudes was desirable (as I think it often is) then the crucial step is to help a group of minders support and reinforce each other. The necessary consequences of a successful course for childminders *must* be some kind of autonomous childminders group. (Rathbone Society: 1976: 20)

I would argue that, at best, an ongoing group is a prerequisite of a course rather than a consequence. It gives the minders the experience and self-confidence to tackle new areas and new people: the children are more at ease in a familiar setting, allowing the minders greater concentration and there will be more leisure to branch out into new fields. One of the most popular classes during the Brixton course was a pottery workshop which some tried to continue later. The Manchester minders enjoyed regular slimming/keep fit sessions.

Support inevitably becomes education and vice versa and vocational education for mature students, especially in an area of female expertise such as this, is peculiarly reliant on the pooling and discussion of knowledge rather than on formal teaching which can so easily be dismissed if it clashes with your own hard-won beliefs and practices.

Notes

1 The Nurseries and Childminders Regulation Act, 1948, amended by the Health Services and Public Health Act, 1968.
2 One or two sessions were actually held at the college, e.g. the one on cheap and nutritious meals, which required a cookery classroom.
3 Conspicuously absent from the list are parents who, of course, are at work during the day and tired at night – we never satisfactorily solved that one.

8 The Sheffield Clothing Co-operative – PREMTOGS
Beverley Evans

In 1980-81 Chaucer Adult Education Centre in Sheffield started a two days a week 'Sew and Sell' class with a crêche provided. Four needlework teachers were employed to teach basic techniques and maintain a minimum standard. Some twenty women joined the class, but it dropped to twelve regular attenders. After the first term we had a variety of skills and decided on a Christmas Fayre. Although goods were sold, we realised they were the wrong items for the district where we were selling them.

The following term we further improved upon and gained more skills, and had discussions on what we could sell and where. One of the girls had been a Nursing Sister in an intensive care baby unit and she pointed out the lack of tiny clothes. We also noticed that the physically handicapped had difficulties with clothes. We researched the potential market by visiting hospitals and schools.

In spring 1981 Granada TV ran a competition for co-operatives and we entered our idea of producing clothes for premature babies along with a set of statistics showing the number of births. After being short-listed, followed by an interview in Manchester, we won £500. This was used to buy two overlocker machines, which we considered most essential to give a professional finish.

We registered as a co-operative under ICOM (Industrial Common Ownership Movement) rules and Sheffield City Council helped with the fee. At this point several women dropped out because they envisaged problems with their income.

Samples of the baby sleeper we produced were sent to various hospitals, but because of lack of response we were forced to take on other sewing work for various educational establishments. We affiliated to the Sheffield Co-operative Development Group and had a stand at the Sheffield Show in 1982 for three days. We advertised in several papers and magazines but there has never been enough response to pay regular incomes. Lack of work has meant more women resigning which has now left two non-worker members and one part-time worker (myself) – a very undemocratic situation.

In the light of the present situation I am faced with several options: (a) closing the co-operative, which I am loathe to do after all the effort of trying to make it work and (b) encouraging new members to join. Without regular work this will be hard. Women are especially hard to convince of their own potential.

Personally, I have been elected on to the Sheffield Co-operative Development Board which tries to help co-operatives with their difficulties, such as arranging for members to go on courses for office management and first aid, advising on insurance to suit their particular circumstances. There are several women's co-operatives in Sheffield: Silver Needles (Community group); Bangladesh Sewing Co-operative; Women's Housing Co-operative, and most successful of all, The Printing Co-operative. Women also are involved in a Bookshop and an Engineering Co-operative, and there is a woman plumber in a co-operative building project. Personal experience encourages me to offer the following advice to women wanting to work together:

(a) try to get members with commitment and enthusiasm;
(b) have several ideas and check the market;
(c) organise the financial situation;
(d) have one member at least willing to do the office work; official forms can be complicated and must be dealt with regularly;
(e) promotion of the service or product by all or one of the members.

The 'Sew and Sell' class was an interesting idea with great potential but unfortunately the only women who responded were on low incomes and required the money immediately. They lacked the commitment and enthusiasm to help promote themselves. This does not mean the idea would not work in another area with a different set of women. Education still has a long way to go to give women the confidence to believe in themselves.

Postscript: In June 1983, Beverly Evans wrote to say that 'PREMTOGS has more or less finished, since there is only me now involved. I have, however tried to pass on the name and registration to local design students but they don't feel ready for it yet. I shall keep looking for suitable premises to take over.'

9 Women and New Technology – Where Are We Going? – A New Course for Women in Liverpool
Rita Cordon and Liz Cousins

It is now clear, despite the wealth of contradictory opinions, that the jobs being most seriously affected by the introduction of new technology are in the service sector. It is in shops and offices – traditional areas of employment for women – that the effect is going to be greatest. We hear all the time that new technology is going to make our lives easier by creating leisure time through labour-saving devices. The disturbing thing would be if this were to occur at the expense of women's hard-won right to a paid job outside the house.

It was a belief in women's right to work for pay and a matching right to good training that acted as starting points in the early days of the Women's Technology Scheme in Liverpool. The Women's Technology Scheme began training thirty women in micro-electronics and computing in the spring of 1984. The development of the scheme provides a good example of how lessons can be learnt from providing good and accessible education for women which can be applied to the provision of training for women.

In July 1982 we undertook a feasibility study looking into the needs for training for women in new technology. We had the debate and good practice which existed in Liverpool through the Women's Education Centre as a stimulus to this work and we worked with certain fundamental principles right from the start. These were:

- that women have the right to work, not just in low-paid, low-status jobs;
- that in order to achieve this women need good training;
- that training in non-traditional areas of employment should be provided in a setting which makes the transition most possible, thus it should be provided in so far as is possible by an all-women staff to an all-women group of trainees;
- that women's domestic responsibilities should be taken into account and childcare be provided on the scheme;
- that high standards of training and educational content should be provided for the women.

In the course of the feasibility study we found that very little training exists for mature women in Liverpool. Perhaps more depressingly, what training does exist pays little attention to what employment might be available at the end of the training. Our commitment to the women who might come on our course made us want to provide a training which might realistically lead to jobs and not merely raise expectations for these to be dashed at the end of the training.

The outcome is a year-long training programme in micro-electronics and computing which will enable women to take up jobs as technicians and maintenance engineers. The Engineering Industry Training Board's Report of 1980 notes that only 2 per cent of technicians are women, a figure that has shown no increase since the 1960s. However, in our discussions with local firms, it became clear that the problem was less one of prejudice against women and more one of women's lack of the necessary level of training. It seems likely that this is one of the few areas where jobs are likely to increase in the future. If women are not trained for them, men will inevitably take them as they have in the past.

We looked towards the European Social Fund (ESF) as a potential source of funding in the first place, because it seemed to offer what is not available elsewhere – large sums of money for training. Perhaps more surprisingly, it has, until 1983 at least, had a special budget for women. The ESF is not without its problems, however, and though for many small groups it represents the only way of getting funding for training schemes, it is not really geared to providing for the needs of such groups. More remains to be said elsewhere about the ESF, how it can be used and what the problems inherent in it are. But here we deal only with two aspects of the work of the Women's Technology Scheme which we feel has helped us work through the maze of bureaucracy connected with the ESF. The first is that we were able to get a grant to undertake the feasibility study. This allowed us to research the employment field, to look at what training already existed, to liaise with local employers and training bodies in designing the course outline, and make the application to the ESF and Inner City Partnership. Since then we have managed to find funding to keep us in post (a job-share). During this time we have continued to liaise with employers, negotiate for other feed-in courses, lobby for funding, and provide courses to raise interest in new technology training among women. The preliminary work is essential and will, hopefully, allow the scheme to start with fewer problems than if we had not done it. The second is that we have been able to persuade Liverpool City Council to provide for a feed-in period to the training scheme. The ESF does not make any provision for getting projects off the ground, yet obviously a great deal of course preparation needs to be done by staff before students actually arrive. Success in getting a grant to cover the wages of the six members of staff for a three-month period prior to the project starting looks like the key development in getting the scheme off to a good start.

Courses such as this are only a small beginning. But a great deal needs to be done if women are to make up the necessary ground in employment. A commitment to providing *real* training is essential. As one local employer we talked to said, 'In future people who don't know anything about computers will be like people who can't read and write today.' There is a need for basic foundation courses in science and technology which will inform women and raise confidence. That is necessary before embarking on training in what has hitherto been a foreign world for so many of us. Vocational training of this kind for women needs to be much more widely available. Otherwise the technological revolution will have the effect of setting the clock back for women.

10 Women and Skill Centres – The Deptford Experience
Madeleine Dickens

In 1982 women formed only 4 per cent of all trainees in government skill centres, but the percentage varies from region to region. There are some sixty skill centres in the country but only four or five are known to have women-only courses. But women do of course, though in very small numbers, join other courses offered in the skill centres. There are many reasons for this: general lack of childcare provision, discriminatory attitudes against women taking up manual and technical skills, particularly in job centres and the attitudes in the skill centres where there is a lack of flexibility in hours and training arrangements.

The women-only manual skills introduction courses at Deptford Skill Centre in South London represents an attempt to challenge and eventually overcome as many of the barriers as possible. The course is seen as a preparation for the Training Opportunities Scheme (TOPS) courses in manual and technical skills. During the ten weeks it lasts, women have the chance to try out a whole range of skills – carpentry, plumbing, various aspects of engineering, motor mechanics, printing, electronics, industrial glass blowing, welding and many others. The main aim of the course is to give women confidence in their ability to acquire such skills and to prepare them as far as is possible for the difficulties they are likely to encounter in taking further training or in working in traditional male-dominated spheres. The trainees are paid £38.00 per week (1984) or the allowance is made up to the level of their previous benefit if this is higher. A small travel grant is payable for women living more than $2\frac{1}{2}$ miles from the centre.

The course has one male instructor – teaching all the skills (male instructors are so versatile!). Even the MSC in the early stages of the negotiations recognised the importance of a woman instructor, but not surprisingly no women rushed to fill the post. In an attempt to counteract this to some extent the centre obtained money from a local college to employ a part-time woman counsellor. Her job is to organise weekly sessions on topics such as sexual harassment and co-operatives as well as giving individual advice on benefits, further training, employment and childcare. In 1983 the local authority gave funding for a full-time worker who has a mediatory and helping role between the students and the Skill Centre staff. This does not minimise the effectiveness of the group support the trainees have created for themselves in what is predominantly a masculine environment.

The wide range of problems the women face can only be tackled by concerted long-term intervention. They have to deal with the prevailing sexist attitudes, and an environment where they are constantly reminded of their presumption in being there at all. They also suffer severely from the institutional pressures: the simulated male workplace, the rigid work discipline (this works wonders for female solidarity).

By 1983 about thirty women had taken the course. Although there have been over one hundred serious enquiries, two-thirds of these women for one reason or another did not take up the course. One of the major problems was lack of childcare facilities, not just for women with children under five, although the appalling inadequacy of nursery provision is serious enough. In fact women with school-age children are also disadvantaged because of the timing of the course from 8.00 a.m. to 3.45 p.m. There is also the perennial nightmare for the mother working outside the home: what to do with children during the school holidays. A group of women interested and involved in the course pushed from the beginning for nursery provision to be made available in the Skill Centres. We realised that problems of childcare had to be made visible and that we had to press for wider recognition, particularly official, of the scale of the problems women face when returning to work or training. There was considerable optimism when the MSC after lengthy negotiations agreed to a nursery being established on the premises for the children of any trainees in the centre. There was a proviso of course, that the money for staff, etc. had to be found elsewhere. After extensive lobbying on the part of the campaigning group, three local authorities agreed to fund the nursery to the tune of £33,000 a year. Euphoria at this apparent breakthrough was, however, short-lived.

Just as the advertisements for staff were to go into the papers, the Manpower Services Commission (MSC) started to employ delaying tactics. These were quickly followed by rumours that the nursery had been blocked at ministerial level. A meeting with the Minister for Employment left no doubt that there had been pressure applied on the Manpower Services Commission (MSC) to renege on its negotiations and that the nursery would not be set up. It was later officially turned down. Arguments that the Manpower Services Commission (MSC) would not be involved in any financial commitment to the nursery appear to have been superseded by concern at the highest government level that the establishment of childcare facilities at a Skills Centre might set a precedent. Heaven forbid, after all, that women with children be encouraged in the present economic climate to have any aspirations, let alone the chance to acquire manual or technical skills. The official line at all levels of the Manpower Services Commission (MSC) and in the Department of Employment remains that women should not be insulated from the 'real world of work'. In other words, if they are unable to make their own childcare arrangements, even during training, they should remain in the home.

After the Manpower Services Commission (MSC) had turned down the nursery, negotiations continued with the three local authorities who had originally promised it funding. They were asked to fund childminders for women with both pre-school and school-aged children.

Most of the women working in Britain in manual and technical trades up to now have been single, had college or university education, and almost all have been white. The Deptford course in its short life has attracted women from different backgrounds. Six of the thirty women who have taken the course have been black and five of the students have had children. Nearly 50 per cent have had no post-school education or training, and none had considered a training in manual or technical skills until learning about the course. The great interest in the nursery can be seen by the fact that over 800 signatures were collected in a petition from one borough alone. If any further vindication was needed the Manpower Services Commission's (MSCs) own research at the national level into women's lack of participation in Skill Centres (yet to be published) has shown that childcare is a major issue. The potential for such a course, even in the alienating environment of a Skill Centre, remains enormous. It is a tragedy that the women-only course at Deptford represents an anomaly which is unacceptable to the government at a time of the increasing privatisation of Skill Centre provision and the drastic cuts in all kinds of adult training.

In 1983/4 there is a projected 40 per cent cut in Skill Centre budgets in the London region. This trend is shown by the Manpower Services Commission's (MSCs) refusal to fund a women's course at the Lambeth Skill Centre in South London, after not only lengthy but seemingly positive negotiations. There are also strong indications that the Deptford course will not be allowed to continue after April 1984. It will not, however, go down without a fight.

Postscript. In November 1984 the MSC agreed to a nursery at the Skill Centre, but the future of the Centre itself still remains uncertain.

Section 4 – Women in Centres

11 Chinese Women on Merseyside
Anne Chiew Yean Khoo, Chinese Women's Welfare Worker

The Tai Shen Chinese Play Assocation is a voluntary organisation which has in the past provided a support service to the Pagoda of Hundred Harmony, Chinese Community Centre, in Liverpool. It is a touring company aimed at promoting traditional Chinese culture in this country. Since its establishment in 1976, the Association has put on regular performances at the Centre and many other theatres throughout Britain. The Association also promotes Chinese music and it has recruited students to learn various Chinese instruments with the intention of forming a Chinese orchestra. Under a Manpower Services Commission scheme, the Association has, for the past three years, sponsored a Chinese Women's Welfare Worker. During my year as a Chinese Women's Welfare Worker, my primary role has been to look into the needs of Chinese women on Merseyside.

Most of the women who seek the centre's help are mothers with young children. Many of them are new to this country having often arrived to join their husbands who are working here. On the other hand, there are also numerous women who have lived in this country for a much longer period of time. In both cases, the women have some things in common. They are mainly housewives, often quite isolated, and speak little or no English. Hence the language barrier and, to some extent, the cultural differences are the predominant difficulties of all these women. Furthermore, many of them are unaware of the facilities available to them. My role is invaluable here in helping to make them aware of the social and educational facilities available.

A large number of cases which I deal with are of a medical kind.

For instance, I have accompanied mothers to ante- and post-natal care services, helped those who wished to have abortions and accompanied others to dental and similar appointments. I also advise those mothers who are eligible to apply for and claim child benefit and supplementary allowances.

The availability of English language classes on Merseyside for those seeking to learn a second language has been brought to the attention of these women. A few of them have shown interest and attended the classes outside, with women of other ethnic backgrounds. The response has been poor because these women were shy at attending classes with other people outside the centre. Therefore, since April 1983 the centre has run its own twice-weekly English language classes. The classes have taken off very well, with about ten regular students. The centre positively encourages women to learn English so that they are able to communicate with others and especially their own children who attend school in Britain. However, not all who come to our centre attend the classes, but they still come if they require assistance.

These housewives regard the centre as a Chinese advice bureau. It is a place where they can come to seek help for their problems and also to talk to the welfare worker in confidence. This is important, as some of these women have no close family relations in this country to whom they can turn to in times of crisis. There are also those women who do have relations here but who are not on good terms with them. Hence the centre is viewed as a neutral place.

The numerous cultural activities held at the centre, for example the Chinese orchestra, variety concerts and pantomimes, have also assisted in encouraging these members of the community, amongst others, to visit the centre. Such activities have enabled some of them to participate in one way or another and have also provided opportunities for them to meet and make friends with other users.

There is also a Chinese Folk Dancing group who meet regularly at the centre. Many of the women in this group have been to school in Britain from an early age, whilst others have been educated in this country for several years. In general, many of the women in this dance group have had some form of higher education and some have permanent jobs. Interviews with these women have indicated that they are generally more independent and self-reliant as individuals than the housewives and mothers. Furthermore, those who have gone through higher education and have achieved better qualifications tend to have higher aspirations. The desire for a career is more important to them and they have greater choices available, especially in the way they lead their lives. For instance, they have some choice in deciding on their careers, whether to continue their jobs after marriage, perhaps defer marriage or even defer having a family. In comparison, the traditional Chinese values stress the importance for woman of being married and bearing children, especially male children in order to perpetuate her husband's line of descent. That was seen as the woman's primary and most valued role in life. One can see a gradual erosion of these traditional values in recent years. Some members of the group have stated that their parents have encouraged them to do well at school in order that they can continue their education. This leads to a job and economic independence.

The centre is an important base for the women in the folk dancing group. It is a place where they can get together, especially at weekends, and maintain their cultural origins. They would like to see a tradition of folk dancing established at the centre that starts from an early age, not only for the present, but also for the future generations of Merseyside's Chinese. In addition, Chinese culture is upheld by mother-tongue classes in Mandarin and Cantonese that are held in the evenings at the centre.

Some differences between the two groups of women may be drawn. Most of the housewives are older than the women in the dance group. To draw on the difference between the two groups, one needs first of all to understand the significance of Chinese traditional values on the former's early socialisation process. The important role a woman holds in the domestic sphere has largely been instilled into her by her mother; for instance, Chinese girls at home were expected to help with household chores and were taught to cook and sew. The ability to manage a household in preparation for her future home was seen as the norm. As a result, the importance of wider education was played down in the case of daughters compared to sons. This is because higher education was considered unnecessary for girls as they would eventually get married and bring up a family. Therefore this group of women started off with a disadvantage over the young women by being less highly educated and motivated.

The women in the dance group have benefited from the gradual erosion of traditional Chinese values and the growing awareness of the importance of education for girls. Parental attitudes, values and encouragement are crucial for a child, especially in her most formative years. Besides, those women who are educated in Britain from an early age are exposed to a wider choice of activities. The western approach to education encourages students to analyse and reason facts for themselves and not to accept anything blindly. In comparison, Chinese children are traditionally taught to respect and obey, unquestioningly, their parents and their teachers at school.

As an indication of change, some of the housewives who have lived in Britain for a while have taken part-time employment to help their economic position, especially in the catering trade. Their children are usually looked after by grandparents or sent to the pre-school nursery at the centre.

It can be seen that the environment and background the women come from relate to their educational and social aspirations. Ultimately this leads to an improvement in the lives of women. It may be concluded, also, that the Chinese mothers are learning and benefiting in some respects as a direct result of seeking the centre's assistance. This has all been part of the educational process to make the Community Centre a focal point in the lives of the Chinese community, in respect of both social and cultural activities.

12 The Women's Education Centre, Southampton
Pauline Imrie, on behalf of the Women's Education Collective

The Women's Education Centre has been set up to provide a meeting place for women to come and learn about and discuss issues which affect their everyday lives.

Many women reach a point when they realise there must be more to life than their children and housework and look to education as a means of improving their position. Some have missed out on educational opportunities in the past and when, through a change in circumstances, e.g. broken marriage or redundancy of their spouse, they have become the breadwinner, they realise their poor position in the labour market.

But conventional adult education ignores the needs of women themselves. The programme usually offered by local education authorities includes subjects such as cookery, needlework and crafts, which reinforce society's view of women in the role of wives, mothers and homemakers. Although such skills as typing and shorthand are offered, they confirm the narrow range of opportunities available for women. Also the usual programme includes little that would appeal to working-class women who have not had a good basic education.

Because of this lack of provision, the Second Chance for Women course was set up by the Department of Adult Education, Southampton University, in 1979 (see Thompson: 1983). The course is run on one day a week for a year. Unfortunately, there are only forty places each year, about a quarter of the number needed to fill the demand. The women come from a variety of backgrounds and age groups, but all have one common factor – the need to move forward. Many are uncertain of the direction in which to make progress. About half have no academic qualifications at all and have not taken any courses since leaving school, whilst others have CSE and GCE passes. Second Chance offers education in the widest sense to these women, which traditional adult education does not. Over the year we look at and discuss subjects which affect women's lives and consider what sort of society ours is for women today and in the past. There are a few essays to try each term, so women are given the chance to see how they cope with formal study. Some are motivated to apply for higher education or to study 'O' and 'A' levels. Others decide to apply for better jobs.

The Women's Education Centre grew out of the enthusiasm of women attending past Second Chance courses. Faced with a future without the stimulation and support gained from the course, the women realised the need for a permanent base where women's education could be taken seriously and women themselves could be in control of the courses offered and how the centre is run.

The local education authority has let us have the use of a building that is part of a further education centre. We are soon to expand into an adjacent building which will provide a much-needed crèche. Some resources are also provided by the university and WEA. We also have independent funding in the form of a grant from the Equal Opportunities Commission, and from money we are able to raise ourselves. The centre is democratically run by the Collective which meets regularly to decide on issues affecting the centre. The Collective is open to anyone who uses the centre.

In the centre's programme are included all sorts of activities and courses to do with women's lives, e.g. law, politics, history, health, women's rights. We have run car maintenance classes and have plans to start basic plumbing, carpentry and electronics work-shops. We are also concerned with our bodies and emotions and include yoga, self-defence and sexuality workshops in our programme.

The centre is really only just finding its feet, although it has already become a meeting place. Past Second Chance students can keep in touch with each other, and it provides a supportive environment for those who have moved on to higher education. It also attracts women from the professions and mature students who value that support, but who did not need the Second Chance course to establish their personal direction. However, it is important that the centre does not become dominated by one kind of woman, i.e. the better educated, but continues to find different ways of attracting all those women who could benefit from the educational and social aspects the centre has to offer.

Postscript: February 1984

I wrote the above article in spring 1983, when I was part of the Second Chance for Women course. As I have now gone on to full-time education, I am not so actively involved with the centre, but understand that the situation is very much the same as last year; some courses continue to be funded by WEA and the university. Tutor costs for other courses have to be covered by fees and fund-raising activities. The spring 1984 programme includes two Second Chance courses, with optional Maths, Women's Drama, Women's Dance, Sociology, Women's History, two House Maintenance courses, and Women's Self-Defence.

13 The Totnes Women's Centre – A Personal Experience
Diana Derioz

The Totnes Women's Centre in South Devon grew from three consciousness-raising (CR) groups and some of us wanted to start up our own craft business and co-operatives. Carol, with a grown-up family, who had always wanted to run a bookshop, was able to buy a building in the centre of the town from her husband and his partner. And so the Women's Centre was born in 1981; from the start all decisions were collectively made by the members and users of the centre. Finances are precarious, since the centre depends on rents from the workshops and individual contributions from users and members. We have not so far received any grants from outside. The following table is typical of one month's income and expenditure. We have put this in as it may be helpful to other women who plan to start their own centres.

Incomings Rents	Per Month	Outgoings Payments	Per Month	
Schmocks	75.00	Maintenance/rent	72.00	
Green Shoes	52.00	Rates	91.18	
Hazel Selina	32.00	Water rates	10.00	
Woolnut	36.00	Electricity	30.00	apx.
Avice	16.00	(mainly metered)		
Ruth	8.00	Insurance	9.00	
Bookshop	Nil	Petty cash	10.00	apx.
Groups (30p per person)	24.00 apx.			
Canteen	20.00 "			
TOTAL	260.00	TOTAL	222.18	

Note: Schmocks has now moved out, being so successful, but in place is Charlotte paying £40.00 per month and Lesley £32.00.

One decision the Collective made was whether men should use the centre. So far men can come in and buy from the businesses, but the women's room and canteen are women only, and so are evening meetings.

The first year in the centre, which we had painted and decorated together, was full of energy and enthusiasm. We had three Consciousness-raising (CR) groups, a women's health group, two writers' groups, a self-help therapy group, a peace group, and we ran a free pregnany-testing service and produced a centre newsletter. Christine installed the canteen and cooked vegetarian food for us, but found it hard to make it pay. We all met Friday evenings and discussed centre business for an hour before splitting off into our CR groups, and new women were introduced into the open group. The businesses were functioning well, and we helped support each other.

By the second year we were settling in well. As only one CR group was operating, the first two having petered out, we decided to have an invited speaker, therapist, or group, to run the Friday evenings, and we advertised these evenings locally. These are some of the topics: An Only Women Press Poetry Reading; a local feminist weaver, Jill Raymond, showing her work and talking about her life; a woman writer, Jane Beeson, reading and giving us advice on how to reach an audience or publisher; a workshop on Mothers and Daughters, run by a trained counsellor, Fiona Green, from London; a slideshow about women artists by Kate Walker, a painter; a local pressure group for nursery education; a dream workshop by Prue Hughes, a therapist; a workshop on the menopause by Pat Kitto, a local counsellor involved in setting up the Totnes Natural Health Centre. We also had a women's weekend, and a peace weekend, and several one-day workshops on sexuality and abortion counselling.

Now we are into our third year, and there have been many changes in our lives. Andrea started doing mail-order smocks, and her business took off so fast she has had to move out into larger premises. This has given two new women opportunity to set up workshops; Lesley, doing china repairs and restoration, and Charlotte, who does printing on to cotton with bright bold designs. Indeed this is what we had hoped would happen; that once a business really started making money, women could move out and allow space for new ventures. Ruth shared my knitwear workshop for a year after leaving college, and has just held her first art exhibition locally, with great success. Hazel is now doing metamorphic therapy, which causes real changes in the way people lead their lives, thus affecting their health radically; and she has also helped to set up a homebirth group, to combat the massive hospitalisation of women for childbirth; Sarah and Alison have expanded their hand-made leather shoe business and are training Lucy to join the co-operative, and Pamela is also working with them. They are also helping to produce a local community newspaper, *The Dart*, which reflects the concerns and airs new ideas within the community.

It is hard to look back and assess the changes that have occurred in my life since I joined the Women's Group without seeming to exaggerate the influence it had on the way I live. Yet it is true that all the choices I have made arose from the discoveries we made together over the eighteen months that our group lasted, and continue to make within the Women's Centre we set up together, and in which I have my knitwear business, supporting myself and my three children.

I was then thirty-three, and the mother of a baby girl and two boys of nine and thirteen, from a French marriage which had broken up three years previously. I taught part-time, both crafts and English to foreign students, but was finding a lack of purpose and creativity in the way I lived, and was increasingly frustrated at finding myself in the position of a mother at home, just as I was beginning to explore my freedom from marriage. I had tried on several occasions to work co-operatively, and was involved in setting up with a mixed collective of teachers, a School of English, but I constantly found that my ideas were being strongly criticised by the men, and although I felt, confusedly, that there was some kind of power struggle taking place, I received no support from the other women. It was only once I started to work with feminist women who were making it their priority to support each other, that I realised how creative women are in the way they build up on ideas together, and reach a consensus of opinion, instead of opposing and dominating each other. Together we looked at our lives, with or without men, our relationships with our mothers and fathers, and our friendships with women. We stopped blaming ourselves for failure to achieve perfect marriages, or for letting down women friends in the past. It became clear as we repeatedly delineated a common experience, that we were brought up to an impossible and ultimately impoverishing task of servicing men and children, doing all their caring for them, training them in their roles as women and men, in exchange for economic dependence and society's demeaning approval. This all seems commonplace with the wealth of feminist literature today, but it broke over me like a tidal wave, releasing anger, distress, and many other depressed emotions that I had held in check for years, and this liberation gave way to new energy and ideas.

The self-help therapy group I was involved in for a year led to enormous changes in the patterns of behaviour I had set up over the years; I was forced to look at my competitiveness, my aggressive energy (formerly used to getting my own way in a man's world), the way I made people dependent on me so that I felt needed and thus validated. I learnt to let go of resentment, instead of harbouring it, by expressing my feelings more honestly and openly. I explored my excessive anxieties about money, which provided a focal point for other problems, thus serving as a carpet to sweep them under. This all gave me courage to take more space for myself to be creative in. I plan to set up a new type of co-operative of designer knitters, hopefully all feminist women. We would provide work for knitters who would be women who needed part-time, well-paid work, and who would have the option to design when they wanted it. Any profits could go into machines, publicity and selling, and all members would be paid equally. I am also looking for a shop to set up a co-operative with Green Shoes (Sarah and Alison), which would sell other women's work, and provide them with an outlet. Hazel and I have started a parent-run co-operative pre-schooling project with a group of others who feel as we do that the changes we are making must above all be communicated to our children so that they can avoid the cycle of dependency and lack of initiative that most schools deal in.

As it is we find ourselves having to take on too much responsibility for the running of the centre, among too few of us, and we sometimes feel confused about expectations when new women move in, not least because we can't expect feminist women to apply for workspace all the time – and our definitions of feminism vary anyway. We just have to hope that constant discussion amongst us will decide controversial decisions such as the women-only canteen and meeting room. At the moment the Collective is formed by any women who want to participate, and by the women who have businesses in the centre, and the jobs of Treasurer and Secretary are rotated between us. We all pay rent for our workshops, and women who are just setting up can get a half-rent support for as long as they need it. We have not managed to get any sort of grant for the centre, which means it is largely financed by the rents, and we can't afford a part-time worker or co-ordinator, although we are looking into placements from colleges. The rates we pay are very high because we have a shop front and are in the town centre, but if we have a surplus, we send it to help other women's projects.

I hope I haven't made it all sound too easy. I have not mentioned the many problems we have had within our groups; we threaten each other when we change or when we demand too much commitment, and many women have left groups because of this. Open conflict is difficult, and it is hard to give up our old manipulative ways which served us so well when dealing with men. Success is scary and brings up feelings of inadequacy and insecurity. And meeting women daily who are isolated and dependent and who need so much in the way of support, can lead us to play always the strong nurturing roles to the detriment of our friends and children, and often exhausts us. Yet the humour, the warmth, the caring and the commitment to each other, and to change that I see in the women around me, fill me with hope for our future, and that of our children.

Note: For a fuller description of the many activities and initiatives of the Totnes Women's Centre see *FAN* (*Feminist Arts News*), no. 8, 1983, 'Gaining Our Ground'.

Section 5 – Processes

14 Women and Education Group, Manchester

Joy Rose, on behalf of the Women and Education Collective

Women and Education is a feminist collective, conceived at the Women's Liberation Conference in Bristol in 1972 in a workshop on education. Originally the intention was production of a newsletter with lists of contacts, publications and reports of conferences and initiatives. The original hand-duplicated newsletter has matured into a termly magazine *Women's Education Newsletter* collated and printed by 'Amazon', a local feminist press. We meet several times during its production, initially to determine a focus for the next issue and to conscript articles, and then, as a spur to produce promised articles, we meet to read through completed submissions. The news section is a continuous process of gathering information from all sources around us. A couple of weeks typing, a weekend dedicated to laying out the pages and the magazine should be ready for printing. Despite disruptions to this schedule, the magazine usually appears. Finally, mailing to subscribers or delivering to distributers completes the procedure.

The collective has flourished and grown into more than a production team. Over the last ten years the shape has changed. The founders maintain contact and occasionally contribute, but have relinquished responsibility, whilst new faces appear and disappear, our numbers perpetually changing. Our social events reunite current and past members, drawing women from miles around who, no longer active within the group, have become and remained friends.

I arrived at a discussion meeting six years ago prepared to offer my time and skills, arrogantly self-congratulatory, proud of my commitment. I wonder now that I ever dared call myself a feminist. I was impressed by the stirring debate which I remember was on girls' schools versus co-education. The overriding feeling was that mixed schools were merely boys' schools with girls in them, as Eileen Byrne so aptly phrased it (Byrne: 1978: 133) but division occurred over whether our energy should be concentrated on making improvements there or campaigning for a return to single-sex schooling. These monthly discussion meetings are open to all women interested in education, not just the Collective. The topics have been varied and have included: Subject Options and Careers, Contemporary Feminist Literature, Science in Soviet Schools, Eliminating Sex-Stereotyping through Drama, Youth Training Schemes, Asian Women and Western Education.

At that first meeting my interest was aroused, but I was shocked when, later, discussion turned to chat over tea and cake. 'How can women spare time from revolutionary activity for baking and frivolity?' I wondered. Yet in retrospect the time to be human and concerned about each other's lives was what characterised the group. Our meetings, whether for business or discussion, are informal and amiable. There is always time for support and advice, often time for laughter. Over the years women in the group have married, divorced, given birth, been bereaved, been promoted, made redundant, been published, changed political affiliations, dropped out of teaching, followed courses of study and even returned to teaching. The Collective has endured and has been enriched by these events, because we believe that women's own experience is paramount and we work from that basis, rather than from the findings of academic research. Some of us appreciate the complementary value of such research and recognise it as a necessary means of reaching beyond a feminist ghetto. We are frequently invited to report the findings of research, to review books and pamphlets and, though we have not sat down and worked them out, our criteria have usually been: Is it direct and easily readable? Does it relate to our own experience?

Arising from this is our rejection of mystification and the role of the expert. Whilst recognising that individuals have areas of knowledge with which they are familiar, and practical experience, no one has total or specific responsibility for any area. Working together in this way has allowed the opportunity to explore and develop new ideas, but also one woman's absence does not mean the loss of a vital cog in the machine. We have no formal structure.

Decisions are taken collectively and somehow, though each of us is different, we reach a consensus without pain or pressure. We fit comfortably together, yet we hope we have avoided being exclusive, and new women do seem to feel welcome enough to stay. Domestic, career and political demands make it inevitable that women drop in and out of our workforce. Our understanding and tolerance when these pressures undermine a woman's commitment have kept us going. However, several women have, at different times, found themselves nudging us along, and felt it to be an oppressive role.

Lack of an administrative structure is not always efficient. As well as subscriptions to the magazine, and requests for speakers at conferences, we are inundated with letters from women anxious to retrain, but not knowing how to start, queries from students of women's studies, enquiries about reading material from young women discovering sexism for the first time, and pleas for help and support from isolated teachers combating sexism in the staffroom and the classroom. Unanswered mail piles up. Typing for the newsletter is an onerous chore that invariably slows down its production. We recently discussed applying for a local authority grant to employ a worker, but were reluctant to saddle someone else with the tedious work. We are also in doubt about the level of involvement, and understanding of the issues, that we could expect from a paid worker. The most difficult obstacle, however, was whether the separation of tasks and specialisation was compatible with collective organisation. Working together has, perhaps, kept us together. The problem remains.

A notable aspect of the group is the variety of political views and affiliations of the individuals within it. For a while we defined ourselves as feminist and socialist, but the latter description has since been dropped, though we do embrace many socialist principles. We share the belief that feminists must continue to fight for more and better education for women in all classes, for equal and non-sexist education in schools and colleges, for fairer conditions of work and greater security for women employed in education. This struggle cannot be left to any other organisations, or school managements, or trade unions, or the Equal Opportunities Commission, nor can we wait for a socialist revolution.

One of our most successful ventures was a non-sexist teaching day attended by 115 people from the north-west, approximately one-fifth of whom were men. Workshops were held on Science, Creative Writing, The Media, Teacher Training, Children's

Literature, Art, Pre-School, Women's Studies and Publishing. Another success was our special student issue of the magazine, no. 20 (Autumn 1980), which was allocated Equal Opportunities Commission funds for the free distribution of copies to all institutions of teacher training. This bumper issue, which included articles on all aspects of the curriculum, in-service training, the career structure for women, a board game, a bibliography and a useful address list, sold out two print-runs, over two thousand copies.

How optimistic are we that progress is being made? Since the Manchester Collective began many other women and education groups have been established in Britain: in Sheffiield, Brighton, York, London, Bristol, Nottingham, Glasgow and Edinburgh. A network of communication about non-sexist and anti-sexist initiatives has arisen, such as the Campaign Against Sexism and Sexual Oppression in Education, the Campaign to Impede Sex-stereotyping in the Young, and the Schools Council Newsletter on redressing sex differentiation in schools. Interventionist projects are in operation to discover effective strategies for change, such as Girls Into Science and Technology (GIST) (*Women's Education Newsletter* no. 23 Summer 1982), and the Thameside Initiative (*Women's Education Newsletter* no. 24 Winter 1982). Local education authorities have acknowledged that inequalities do exist, for several have started anti-discrimination policies. Yet, to be realistic, are schools implementing these ideas? More important than policy statements is money to replace and supplement textbooks, pressure on headteachers to recognise the problems and put policies into practice, in-service training, and working parties in schools to oversee their own practice. The elimination of sex-stereotyping and the ensuing inequalities in schools will be perceived by many teachers as an added burden, in the face of daunting classroom pressures with inadequate resources, whilst others regard it as a very low priority. It will take several years before we eradicate the need for collective action amongst women.

15 The Workers Educational Association (WEA) and Women's Education

Ally Jones (in a personal capacity), Editor, WEA Women's Studies Newsletter, *1980-83*

In 1903 the Workers Education Association (WEA) was established with the prime aim of extending educational access to working people. In its early days it provided opportunities for members of the working class to study at University level (the tutorial class); encouraged women students by paying special attention to their needs; linked in with the trade union movement for the education of their members from 1919; and was one of the main pressure groups for the extension of free education for school children and adults prior to the 1944 Education Act. The WEA was a pioneer in the education of the working classes and early in its history recognised the special needs of women. Indeed the opening statement of a special and innovatory leaflet, *Women in the WEA*, issued in 1912, states:

> If the WEA is to gain any substantial victory in its campaign against ignorance and injustice men and women must be fighting side by side . . . . ; so of all the special efforts the WEA is making today, perhaps none is more important than the special effort it is making on behalf of women. (WEA Northern District Reprint: 1982: 9)

In 1912 the need for women-only classes due to the 'reservedness' of some women members was recognised, and so was the necessity for the setting up of special women's sections to fit in with women's domestic responsibilities. Women's sections were recognised as doing missionary work to attract 'the people who perhaps bring no book learning with them, but who bring something we want far more and that is the experience, and insight, and sympathy that are bred of struggle' (WEA Northern District Reprint: 1982: 11).

However, after such an encouraging start the needs of women were submerged by other issues. By 1916 the National Women's Officer who had been appointed in 1910 had left and was not replaced, and the Women's Advisory Committee also had ceased to meet. (Linda Shaw, 'A Brief History of the Progress of Women's Education in the WEA', in *Essays on Women's Education*). It was not until the early 1970s that women's education and women's studies became an issue again within the WEA. The struggles over this have left us, in 1983, less advanced than we were in 1912.

It is necessary to understand the organisation of the WEA in order to see how this has happened. The only national adult education organisation in Britain, it began with a liberal and democratic view of education that has been influential in the formation and practice of its policy and work. It is a voluntary movement and student controlled, with a few paid officials and tutors. Its democratic structuring, running from the elected secretary of the local branch through elected delegates to the District Council, and from there to the National Executive Committee (NEC), means that grassroot ideas and proposals work slowly and cautiously through the organisation to become part of the national WEA policies. Additionally there is a continuing and often fruitful tension between the twenty-one districts and the National Office and its committee; between centralisation and local autonomy. Some of the districts will fight change which is at the expense of efforts to progress nationally. Furthermore, as many of the responsible jobs at the local voluntary level, such as branch secretary and treasurer, tend to be very time-consuming; there is a tendency for the majority of elected representatives to be older people. Unfortunately, some of them are cautious and often against change which they feel may politicise the movement. This means they are often in conflict with the radical ideals and hopes of the younger student members and employees. Also there is the usual contradiction, as exists within other organisations, that, although the majority of students and branch activists are women, their numbers and visibility recede as men become more prominent in the higher strata of the hierarchy on the policy-making district councils and the national committees. Likewise the three full-time national officers, and nineteen out of the twenty-one district secretaries are men.

It is only by putting the WEA within this context that one can understand why, despite the efforts made by supporters of women's studies for the last ten years, relatively little progress has been made in influencing or changing the actual policy-making structures. This is in despite of the lead that the WEA gave at local levels, in the 1970s in pioneering women's education before both the universities and the LEAs. From the early days of the women's liberation movement, in response to ideas and requests from groups of women, local branches of the WEA have put on a wide range of Women's Studies and Women's Education classes.

In 1977 the *WEA Women's Studies Newsletter* was started to collect and circulate experiences and ideas from tutors and students active in the new type of courses for women. Typically and in the best of WEA traditions, the *Women's Studies Newsletter*, the first in the UK, was started on the initiative of Carolyn Brown, a woman student from a local branch in the Midlands. It was edited, duplicated and despatched almost single-handed in the early days by Carolyn, growing from 300 copies to some 800, and was financed precariously through individual and district subscriptions. As

Carolyn said, in 1979, at a WEA National Conference on Women's Education: 'The WEA had done a lot for me and I wanted to do something in return, and also because I thought the WEA was a great organisation' (WEA Report: 1979: 11). Gradually the production of the *Newsletter* became too heavy a burden for one person to produce voluntarily and unpaid with no financial backing, and efforts were made within the WEA to get more support. The WEA was proud of this *Newsletter*, which had become nationally known and had shown the WEA in the forefront of a vital and new self-help education movement, women's studies. It was time to persuade the WEA to translate its recognition of the *Newsletter*'s national impact into financial and administrative backing.

The problem of getting support for financing and editing the *Newsletter* were interlinked with the struggle by women to create a post for a National Women's Education Officer. Many WEA members were uneasy about what they interpreted as the separatist tendencies and subversive direction of women's studies classes. This led to recurring jokes about men's studies, and a reluctance to positively support these initiatives. However, the 1979 biennial conference instructed the National Executive Committee and its officers to investigate ways of funding a women's education post. But the will did not seem to be there to get this done as a priority. The opportunity was lost by not taking up the vacant fourth National Officer post for this purpose: it was abolished and the money used to improve the salaries and status of other employees as the WEA is perennially short of funds. Carolyn Brown resigned from editing the *Newsletter*, and responsibility for this was taken over by the newly created Women's Education Advisory Committee (WEAC), a sub-committee only in the WEA structure.

WEAC is only an *advisory* committee within the WEA and is dependent on the support of the WEA nationally, in particular the National Executive Committee, which has not always been forthcoming. However, despite this some progress has been made. A few districts have established new tutor-organiser posts for women's education; district schools have been held to exchange ideas and to encourage greater participation by women; a national conference on how to provide childcare, covering both financial and organisational problems took place in September 1982; and the first in-service training conference for women's education was held in July 1982.

However the *Newsletter* is still being edited voluntarily, and we have not yet got an officer with national responsibility for women's education. What has happened is that those Districts sympathetic to women's education have progressed in leaps and bounds. In the districts unsympathetic to women's studies there has been relatively little change. Those women who previously found access to classes difficult are still in the same position. Until a national women's officer is appointed to co-ordinate the work, it is difficult to envisage much further progress being made throughout the country.

1983 should have been the breakthrough for women's education in the WEA. The Department of Education and Science, which is a major source of funding for the WEA, had stated that it was up to the districts to fund any new projects at national office and that they could use their grant accordingly. Hence, at the WEA biennial conference in May, there was a resolution calling for a new full-time post at national office with major responsibility for women's education which would be funded through a levy from the districts. For the first time ever the National Executive Committee supported this motion, but it was rejected by Conference. Looking back, it now seems that many opposed this resolution because it was seen as a threat to district autonomy, and that it would strengthen national office at the expense of the districts. The districts that supported the resolution were mainly those who already had thriving women's studies courses and groups; arguably such districts would not have benefited so greatly from the proposed appointment. It would be naive to think that opposition was based only on the central versus local district autonomy issue. It is clear that much of the opposition also came from a continuing mistrust of women's studies courses. There are still many within the movement who do not think that there is any need for special or different educational provision for women, and see women's studies as discriminatory. The answer to this has to be 'Yes, of course it is discriminatory'; this is an essential move for a period of time in order that women may become more equal. It is merely correcting the balance of a society that has oppressed women over many centuries and it will allow women to take their rightful place.

The conclusions which can be drawn from this case study are threefold. In the first place many of the difficulties of getting women's education and women's studies accepted within the WEA can be compared to the struggle to get trade union studies accepted. Similar suspicions were initially voiced against trade union education and indeed, still are to some extent. It has been argued that trade union studies are training because they have to be approved by the TUC, and not education. They are somewhat alien to WEA democratic traditions of local branch control as they are organised at district level. However trade union studies have financial backing from the TUC, providing a steady income for the WEA's always precarious funds. Women's studies have had no such financial and influential backing to assist their acceptance. Without such support they will always be vulnerable.

Secondly, the rejection of the motion to fund a full-time National Women's Education Officer by a levy from districts at the 1983 biennial conference, even though this was supported for the *first time* by the National Executive Committee, was because it unfortunately got caught in the continuing power struggle of the centralising tendencies of national office and the local independence of the twenty-one districts. Those who know and work in the WEA argue that a lot can be done *informally* and at a local level within the movement, and that it would be wiser to press changes (i.e. women's studies) forward by these strategies – the non-confrontational model. After all, they argue, women's studies and education had moved a long way into being accepted and tolerated by WEA members since the 1977 biennal conference when the Chairman said, in closing down the debate on women's studies and the appointment of a women's officer: 'We must press on with more important business.'

Finally, this brief case history highlights the difficulty, and often the unvoiced hidden opposition, of trying to change organisations and to get more women involved in the power structure despite some men being genuinely liberal and supportive of this struggle by women. Ultimately the WEA survives – and eventually thrives – on the challenges from its grassroots, over half of which are women.

16 Liverpool Women's Education Centre
By Themselves

Introduction

A women's education centre in Liverpool came into being as an idea when the special needs of women in education were recognised by adult educators, and a proposal was put to the Inner City

Partnership Scheme for a large education centre which would include a women's education centre.

The building has not materialised. What exists at present is a network of women working in colleges, with the local authority, and in voluntary organisations (virtually all professional educators), who look at issues affecting women in education, and see if action can be taken. Sometimes at the monthly meeting only a few are there, but the network can be quickly alerted and used. Earlier in our existence, we applied for funding for workers, unsuccessfully; and thought of applying recently to the Manpower Services Commission (MSC) for workers, but when we talked it through, we realised that we weren't ready to be employers.

Specifically we have:

- compiled and distributed a woman's guide to education on Merseyside (overwhelmingly successful) (*There's More to Life Than Housework – A Guide to Women's Education* Liverpool, Undated);
- developed a number of courses in different areas and centres on women's issues and women's studies;
- run a day school on different courses for women.

On a regular basis, we act as a campaign and pressure group – for example, over the question of childcare in colleges. We also act as an informal network to provide educational advice.

What now follows are three brief 'case studies' to illustrate some of the difficulties we have met with in trying to have 'education for women':

1 Feminism in one tech?
2 Working 'with' the system.
3 Cost of providing a nursery.

Feminism in one tech?[1]

The college where I teach is historically one where Liverpool boys in the engineering trade went to study. Some people in the area still call it the 'boys' tech. Local businessmen, politicians and college management form the twenty-strong Board of Governors. The only female on the Board is the Student Union representative. In a religiously divided community (subtle, but it's there) the college is said to be Catholic. It's not overt, but most of the college hierarchy and a large proportion of staff are Catholic and people joke that you need to be one to 'get on'. There is only one woman above the basic lecturing grades on the teaching staff, and until four years ago the only women teachers in the college were a couple in the General Studies department.

In 1979, that department got a new head who foresaw the decline of the college's traditional work – training apprentices for local industry – and appointed a lot of new staff, younger, more liberal and with a fair proportion of women, to teach on Manpower Services Commission (MSC) work and adult education. That's how I found myself in 1980 teaching women's studies on a course called 'New Opportuities for Women' (NOW), which was aimed at women who wanted to return to work or study after a break because of domestic responsibilities.

Three years on and sixteen courses later the four of us who form the course team have worked together with a solidarity and harmony that is a great source of satisfaction to us. We have taught several hundred women, many of whom have made real positive changes in their lives. We constantly question what we do, continually trying to improve the course in line with our perception of the needs of our students. The course has been an acknowledged success and we hope it has been a contribution to the feminist struggle.

Sadly, it is about to end. Two members of the course team have resigned, a third is 'considering her position' and the one who will be remaining will not be teaching women at all in the academic year 1983/84. Several months ago we took the unheard-of and unprecedented step of declining to start a new course in the college when the present one ends. We felt so depressed and demoralised over two particular issues and felt we could not go on until they were resolved.

The first was the playgroup set up at the time of the first NOW course. It has always been unsatifactorily located, financially precarious, and opening on too few days and for too few hours, but in the 1982/3 academic year it deteriorated to the point where women had to leave the college rather than use it, and those who continued to take their children there constantly expressed their anger and bitterness. At the same time, the college principal did not allow us to use an article (photocopied from *Spare Rib*, a magazine to which the college library subscribes!) to illustrate a session on contraception. It had been sent for photocopying and the printroom technician had taken it to the principal. Since 1980, about four other items we have used have been questioned. In further education a principal appears to have control over course content. Nevertheless, to our knowledge, this power has never been used to interfere with any course other than ours.

These two issues coming to a head are what triggered off our decision to withdraw from the course, but they need to be seen against a background of what appears to us three years' of hostility and prejudice towards us and our course and the immediate cries of 'hysterical' and 'aggressive' whenever we fight back. Quite simply we've had enough.

It seems clear to us that many people in the college see women as a 'new market' which can replace the college's old work, and the success of NOW and the 'spin-off' effects on the rest of the college have led them to believe that it can be done. What nobody wants to face are the implications of having more women students – better playgroup provision, attempts to get more women staff, changes in course structure and content, changes in the behaviour of men in the college and so on. The close examination of assumptions, beliefs and material practices that would be needed cannot be contemplated and there will be relief that we are no longer around to press for it. For myself, I shall put all my energies and commitment to women's training and education into helping to set up projects outside the system I work in.

And the 'Tech'? Women's education will continue to expand, 'whether you like it or not', we've been told. The college has ignored women's needs since its inception, so that remark seems to show that it intends to carry on doing so.

Working with the system

During 1982 several part-time courses were set up aimed at women in Garston in South Liverpool. The courses were funded by the Liverpool LEA and the WEA.

The courses were arranged in response to the demand shown by women living in the Garston area and included a New Opportunities for Women course and a Women's History course.

Despite the success of the course, the process of finding premises, arranging publicity and liaising with administrators created difficulties for local women getting the kind of course they wanted. Working 'with the system' is not easy for potential students, as these women found out.

I talked to Margaret who was very involved, with other women, in getting courses off the ground, although not actually paid for this work by the educational providers. She spoke about herself and the reasons for her involvement as well as the problems that came up in working 'with the system'.

ME: How did you get involved in the first place?

MARGARET: I went to the nightschool but all the kids came in with the grown-ups. They were saying, 'Miss, shall I do No. 5 or 6 now?' while we were still doing No. 2. They had a rapport with the teacher – they saw her during the daytime. . . . We wanted something to hold our interest – something that could change according to what the women wanted.

ME: Then a meeting was arranged early in 1982?

M. Yes, about twenty-five people turned up. There were a lot of ordinary people plus about four officials. They were talking in their own jargon, you know, WEA this and LEA that and there's no money for this or that. It frightened the life out of some of us. We argued back but we didn't have a clue really. Some of the women said they wouldn't come again. . . . Then we talked to you about getting tutors and we started to get somewhere with one of the officials.

ME: What happened about finding premises for the course?

M. It was after one of our meetings that we went round the corner to the adventure playground and they said that there was some space upstairs. Before that we tried a community centre but they thought they were full up and didn't get back in touch with us. We had met in the multi-services centre but they were overcrowded. Later we heard that some people were moving out but then never heard any more. The Parents Centre ran courses like pottery but didn't seem to do anything that we were interested in. Everywhere seemed miles away – too far to go if you have a baby. We're really badly off for facilities in this area. . . . There were even problems at the adventure playground. We had to use their crèche worker and the 'Education' said it cost too much. In the end she got paid but we couldn't leave anything on the premises and there wasn't space to break into groups.

ME: Once the NOW course started what other problems were there?

M. Well the enrolments messed up some lessons. They had us like school kids one after the other – sign here, where do you live, which school do you go to – next! – they could have treated us like adults. It took all morning and then they said they'd come down from the college the next week in case anyone new had started! . . . With the next course the radio and the paper got all the dates wrong. We took a lot of trouble with all the publicity and then had to move the class after two weeks – we moved to the place we had originally asked for.

ME: So now everything for the course is sorted out?

M.   We had great hopes with the place where we are now, but they can't tell us for sure how long we can be there. You can't advertise something that might not carry on after a few weeks. . . . A local community officer helped us to fill in forms to get money for premises – we've not heard from him since. . . . We were like newcomers to it all. There's just enough help so it looks like we're being helped but we haven't got what we want. We did this questionnaire to show there is a need. There's three hundred or so replies and they need analysing. . . . Now we are in touch with a councillor. There's been a lot of interest but we're still waiting to hear.

ME: How has getting the course going affected you?

M.   I've made millions of phone calls. It became like a full-time job going along to meetings. It seems all right if you belong to something – but we belong to no one at all – no one could give us any decisions. . . . One time we wanted to post twenty-four letters and it was like 'I'll bring the paper' and 'You can get it typed', but who could get some envelopes?

ME: Could you describe yourself?

M.   Well, I'm a woman of thirty-six who knows there's more to life than housework. I left school at fifteen with absolutely no qualifications. I think your brain ceases to function after all those years – apart from signing your family allowance book. A little bit ¨f education when you want it builds your confidence. I wouldn't be afraid to stand up now and talk at a meeting. . . . I just don't think you should have to travel for education – there shouldn't be the pressure to find the bus fare.

The cost of providing a nursery in a college of further education

The campaign began in autumn 1981 with a working party of staff management and students having meetings and circulating a questionnaire. It took three nights to produce and sank without a trace when the Students' Union Committee resigned at Christmas.

In January 1982 the Principal and Vice-Principal suggested sharing with the nearby poly's nursery. This idea was welcomed, not least I suspect because it's nice to have someone else's institution holding your baby.

Then the cost of sharing was announced – over £1,000 per child per annum – and even the sympathetic were aghast.

'But my girls only pay 30p a morning. . . .'

'I only pay my childminder £15 per week.'

'—— College has a playgroup and it's only 50p a session!'
And the ever-familiar

'Why do they have all these children if they don't want to look
after them?'

The outcry revealed widespread ignorance about distinctions
between different forms of childcare, and even about the semantic
distinction between 'fees' and 'costs'. 'Surely, we could do it more
cheaply ourselves' was the most positive response, so the second
working party began by looking for premises (realising that if we
found them we would have to face a further battle for trained staff
with adequate pay and conditions). In fact we never did find them,
but the search was an eye-opener. Inside colleges it seems the
accommodation needs of the under-fives place them in direct
competition with most staff – ground floor, with separate entrance,
proximity to toilets, kitchen and sleeping place. Clearly the
children's needs were not to take priority, but there was some
unused space which might be adapted, provided this cost nothing!
Top garrets, airless basements and holes under the stairs reflected
widespread assumptions that anywhere you wouldn't dream of
putting a student would be perfectly suitable for a child.

So we extended the search outside of college. Adjacent nursery
class? Full and only half-day sessions. A vacant hospital building?
We wasted hours finding the right bureaucrat to ask, only to be
told, '. . . at the present time – not suitable to consider your
request. . . .' (It's still empty!)

At about this time the local Liberal party were considering
adapting a building being used by part of our college to provide a
luxurious primary school complex, and asked if our students would
want to use the nursery facilities. In the end the plan was ditched,
but not before that section of our college had been rehoused,
inadequately, at a cost of over £5,000. The building now stands
empty and vandalised.

We discussed sharing provision with an unemployed centre in
the area. The standard and flexibility of provision were ideal and
the costs reasonable, but the centre was not viewed favourably by
certain parties on the city council and our Board of Governors. In
fact the averted gaze-and-lowered-eye count could hardly have
been higher if we'd suggested subsidising the nursery with child
pornography . . . (I'll bear that one in mind next year).

The Board of Governors had an ongoing role in this saga. I
submitted two reports and was invited to speak to them on two or
three occasions, each time gaining their unanimous sympathy and

support – but no money – so nobody was really surprised when a number of them voted in the City Council against having even a report on the childcare issue, only four days after they had smiled us their support.

Of course we didn't rely on them, or the LEA. We wrote to Heseltine (then Secretary of State for the Environment) and, some weeks later, received a reply, advising us to try the MSC.

Finally, in December 1982, on the last afternoon of term, the Chairman of Goverors agreed to a limited pilot scheme – six children to be subsidised for two terms in . . . the poly's nursery!

We're now nearing the end of the second term with no agreement for next year. We're getting a new Vice-Principal and Chair of Governors. The next round is about to begin.

Meanwhile the phone system is being replaced. Chosen by bureaucrats, against professional advice, it has lasted a year! It cost about £13,000.

Incidentally, the cost of two terms' nursery subsidy was about the same as the college's 'hospitality' bill for the same period – nothing elaborate – just teas and biscuits and the occasional canteen buffet for various meetings – including the Board of Governors.

Conclusions

These conclusions have been drawn from the case studies, as we hope is obvious.

1 We're now more aware of the need to ask the questions:
   – Who is providing education for women?
   – Why?
   – Who controls it?
2 Education for women isn't significantly changing educational institutions – it's not affecting timetables, course content, ways of relating, methods of teaching. Education for women is regarded as a fringe activity.
3 If attempts are made to change, all kinds of vested interests emerge. Time, patience, tenacity, historical perspective on how long change takes, and a sense of humour would seem vital.
4 If students try to say what kind of provision they want, and how, the system does not seem to be geared to coping with this.
5 What we need in Liverpool is an office within the local authority which has responsibility for the education of women, and for

ensuring that necessary changes are made within the existing structure and all parts of college life.

6 As a group, we need a development worker of our own who has clear responsibility for developing groups and interest. Otherwise 'you don't belong' and development is nobody's clear responsibility.

Note

1 Tech, of course, is a technical college of further education.

17 The South West London Women's Studies Group
By Themselves

Beginnings

The South West London Women's Studies Group met for the first time in November 1981. It began as a joint initiative by the Workers Educational Association (WEA) and the Clapham-Battersea Adult Education Institute (AEI). Lynne Garrett, the AEI Community Education Worker, and Amanda Woolley, a Development Officer with the WEA, had observed a growing interest in the area of 'women's studies' in South West London. The minimal provision that already existed had been started by the WEA, with Women's Health courses and Neigbourhood Women's Studies Group on a Battersea estate. The AEI had provided subjects which traditionally attract women students, such as cookery and dressmaking. Now there were requests coming to both organisations for women's classes in a whole range of subjects from carpentry to literature, and particularly for women's self-defence. It looked as if many courses might be launched in the name of 'women's studies' without there being any local discussion or consensus about what this new subject area was or what we were supposed to be doing with it.

Who should teach it? Should the classes be restricted to women only? What range of subjects would be covered? How could we make its appeal as wide as possible? What limitations might be imposed by working within local authority provision? (Although most people who teach and study in adult education are women, the administration is dominated by men.) Finally, would other women share our interests and concerns?

Our first meeting, advertised through work and personal contacts, attracted about thirty women. Since then the Women's Studies Group has met regularly in Clapham about once every six weeks and there has been a stable core of about twelve women involved from the start. Most of them work in adult education, either full-time or part-time, but several joined because they have a general interest in women's education though they work in other fields. The resultant mixture of backgrounds and interests (for example, in child development, massage, libraries, the law) has proved a healthy resource and basis for our work.

Courses

Initially the group served as an introductory network for women tutors and organisers and interested students. This has enabled joint work and team teaching and has helped us plan and mount our own courses. So far there have been eight: four day-schools, each followed by a short course, on Women's Writing, Women's History, Women and Health, Women and Crime.

From these have sprung longer courses organised by the WEA or the AEI. The Women's Writing Day, for instance, generated at least three follow-up courses, leading one of the organising tutors to comment: 'Such a thorough-going commitment from a one-day affair indicates that we are indeed serving the needs of women in the communities of South London.' Between us the teachers in the group must have been involved in a couple of dozen women's studies courses of different types and many are also working in related fields like Fresh Start, English as a Second Language and Literacy.

As a group we have endeavoured to co-operate with other institutions to further our women's studies programme. These include the WEA, to whom we have become affiliated, the Extra-Mural Department of the University of London, various AEIs and community organisations like the Battersea Arts Centre. The group has no facilities or funds of its own yet, but we do have expertise and an extensive network of contacts. It is not always easy to fit into other bodies' programmes and bureaucracies but this sharing of resources has proved valuable on both sides.

Theory

Early on the group realised that there was a need to develop a
theoretical framework for women's studies teaching, establishing
its aims, content and approach and attempting to deal with the
difficult area of publicity: how to attract students to a new and
potentially threatening subject. Though the classes were taught by
responsible tutors who had thought long and hard about these
issues, we were aware that there was not complete agreeement in
the group on every principle and that our ideas were not
necessarily shared by other people working in adult education. We
needed to clarify the theory behind our practice for ourselves, and
to spell it out for our colleagues.

What emerged from our deliberations was the *Womanifesto*, a
policy statement and discussion paper on women's studies.
Wherever is has been circulated it has attracted interest and
stimulated debate. Yet although the group remains committed to
the ideas contained in the *Womanifesto*, it would be a mistake to
consider it our last word on the subject. Already principles which
seemed radical when it was written – such as the notion that men
should be excluded from women's studies classes – are becoming
accepted and established in some institutions, and there are new
issues to take up. The publicity problem has not been overcome
and we cannot pretend, with the best will in the world, that
women's studies yet reaches a fraction of the students we would
like it to reach, nor that we have successfully overcome the racist,
heterosexist and ageist bias which characterises so much of our
work. But we are aware and we are fighting.

The Women's Studies Group would like to maintain a
continuous theoretical debate, but lack of time prevents this being
undertaken in any formal sense. Our meetings are usually taken up
with practical details like organising classes and reporting on the
activities into which our members put their feminist energies. But
when individuals meet at other times, in the course of work or
socially, these issues do crop up and we have opportunities to
develop our views at conferences and in classes. We hope that the
Womanifesto will be but the first of many such documents that we
produce, as our ideas on teaching women's studies change in line
with changing practice in our own teaching and in the institutions,
educational authorities and society at large.

Feminist input

Because members of the Women's Studies Group come from many different professions and are involved in many different causes, we are all constantly engaged in making a feminist contribution to all our activities quite apart from the women's studies classes which we organise and teach. Obviously the amount and type of feminist input that is feasible varies according to the situation. Most professions and organisations do not operate on feminist principles and women who are lawyers, librarians, teachers within institutions, must make many compromises. They have, however, a unique opportunity to influence some of the power bases in our male-dominated society and often the public as well. The librarian in our group, for instance, has acquired an extensive women's studies collection which is invaluable for our students but also brings books to the attention of people who might not otherwise know about women's studies.

Some of our members are active in political organisations and women's groups of various kinds. Through the women's section of a branch of the Labour party, one woman has been influential in forming Labour party policy on issues like girls' education in the district, the licensing of sex shops and the provision of crèches at AEIs. Another is involved in a Greenham Common support group, and many are active in support campaigns for women's causes such as the fight against the threatened closure of the South London Women's Hospital.

We played an organising part in the national Women's Studies Conference held at Deptford in 1982, sending representatives to the planning meetings and securing a major role for adult education in the workshops and discussions. Out latest endeavour has been to try to put together a series of guides for teachers in non-women's studies adult education courses, on ways in which a feminist approach might be incorporated. So far we have considered history, literature and law. Many of us teach 'straight' adult education classes as well as women's studies anyway and are aware of the problems not only of selection of material and method, but of the very different audiences and the danger of alienating them through exposure to feminist ideas – not to speak of the hostility of other tutors and administrators.

The social role

No summary of the group's activities would be complete without a reference to its social function. Meetings become a pleasure when the participants share common beliefs and goals, and it is no exaggeration to say that for many of us the South West Women's Studies Group provides a refuge, support and validation, as well as a number of close friends. We meet socially and have organised outings to feminist plays and films. The following extracts from papers written by members of the group illustrate its importance in their lives:

> . . . For the most part today, except for isolated phenomena like the Greenham Common occupation, women do not experience active participation in public life. Most of us haven't a public life at all, by which I mean a place in which our various selves can be exchanged, given, taken up and recognised. But for me the South London Women's Studies Group has provided a measure of participation in public life. Along with other members of our group I am interested in helping mount and teach women's studies courses for women that higher or conventional adult education would not reach.

> . . . This group has been important for me personally and professionally. It has re-awakened my interest in history, given me wonderful new friends, encouraged and supported me in taking a more active role in those areas where previously I was too hesitant and lacking in confidence.

> . . . It was really by accident that I came to the first meeting of what became the South West London Women's Studies Group. Here I am actually an anomaly, because everyone else in it is working actively in adult education, but I have been made to feel that even an elderly woman, concerned with infants and peace and fairy stories can, as a thinking woman, make her contribution.

18 New Opportunities for Women – Setting up a course – A personal view
Pat Bould and Clare Manifold, Greenwich Action Group on Unemployment (GAGOU) Women's Group

This account is focused around a course for women in South East London. It was set up by women on one day a week for six weeks in the summer of 1981. Pat was part of the women's group that it grew out of and Clare was chosen by the group to co-ordinate and teach.

We think the most useful thing that we can contribute to this collection is our personal recollection of the process and mechanics of setting the course up. We have not yet, three years on, even begun to collate the feelings of other women who attended or helped to set up the course, but we hope to. We do not intend in this description to minimise or disregard the importance of the individual solutions that the course provided, or did not, for those others who were part of it: some women taking further qualifications – some not; some getting work – some not. But what we mainly want to share here is what happened before day one which we ambitiously timetabled as follows:

10.00 – 12.00 :	Introduction to programme
	– getting to know each other (coffee)
	Discussions on our creative unemployment
	– attitudes and suggestions
	Discussion about the course journal
12.00 – 1.00 :	Free lunch
1.00 – 2.00 :	What is a curriculum vitae?
2.00 – 3.00 :	Everyday Maths and English

Speakers from Lewisham Women's Employment Project

The Women's Group of Greenwich Action Group on Unemployment (GAGOU) began when three women got together in November 1980 and started talking about the difficulty of getting a job and getting the kids looked after properly. We found that once we started talking, there were lots of things about 'work' that were different for us than they were for men: not being seen as potential workers, having to insist that others recognised that we needed to work because we needed the money to live on (nothing to do with 'pins'), and the lack of childcare facilities in our area, to name a few. All this had to be considered when we were talking about our needs as workers and thinking about organising ourselves. We felt it was necessary to have a women's group because it was difficult for the three of us to relate to the formalities of the main GAGOU meetings and we thought other women would be feeling the same. We had sat through those meetings not saying a word, but now we were having some really good ideas about what we wanted. Even things like the language used seemed like a separate women's issue – words like, 'unemployed' and 'claimants' unions' didn't say much to us as it was our *unwagedness* as women that we were concerned about. We felt that the best place for us to be was inside a group like GAGOU, part of it but autonomous at the same time. We wanted space to talk about things on our own terms. We brought all this up in the main GAGOU meetings, as well as the need for a crèche and the timings of meetings to be organised so as not to clash with picking up children. We tried to find new ways of contacting other women to join the group – notices in shops, launderettes, posters in schools. . . .

This was taken from a speech Pat gave at an unwaged people's conference at the Mary Ward Centre, London, in 1981. It gives a good background to what GAGOU Women's Group was thinking at that time. We were raising our consciousness about being unwaged women and 'unemployed' too. It seemed clear that there was some kind of knowledge about, which we needed, to start to change our situations, but we weren't sure what it was.

We held our first public meeting in April 1981, to look at education and training facilities in the borough for women. We linked it with a speaker from the Council's Day-Care Department on childcare provision. Thirty-five women came with six children for the crèche (staffed by men from GAGOU). There were only six under-fives because it was mainly older women who came with school-aged children. They were the ones who wanted to talk about training opportunities and retraining. What kept coming up was the fear of handling the Manpower Services Commission (MSC)-funded Training Opportunities Scheme's (TOPS) tests. We called the next meeting specifically to talk about these tests. What came out of that was the massive lack of confidence that a lot of women felt about being confronted by formal testing procedures after a gap of so many years. For most women it seemed that their experience of initial schooling had been undermining and these tests brought back all the old fears of seeming second-rate, with the added difficulty of now being out of practice and older.

The women's group decided that there was a definite need for something organised by women, that wasn't like school, that could help with confidence training, jobs, money. Whatever it was, we could not cope with it in open meetings. We started to compile a list of training opportunities in South East London. We couldn't find what we needed locally, and public transport to the various education centres that we had heard of was difficult and expensive.

Kathryn, a community worker with the group, told us about something happening in North London at the Kentish Town Women's Workshop. Three of us visited it. Clare had just started working out a study programme there with a group of women focussing on women's opportunities and gave us a copy. We took it back to our group for discussion and started work on designing our own. We decided to start with something short. One day a week for six weeks, 10.00 a.m. to 3.00 p.m. (fitting in with school hours). We wanted a non-threatening brush-up on Maths and English (so we could feel strong enough to face TOPS). We wanted ways of making us look viable on paper (curriculum vitaes for job applications). We wanted to practise interviews, we wanted speakers from a trade union (workers' rights), a law centre (benefits), the MSC (TOPS), Lewisham Women's Employment Project (what other women were doing). We also fancied seeing what the inside of a college looked like and wanted to visit a local resources centre (so we would know how to publicise other things). We wanted to see word processors and computers. We thought it would be a good idea to keep a course journal to keep track of how things were going. We planned all this and more to be fitted into six days.

We had to pay for it somehow. A local community centre (the Clock House, Woolwich Dockyard) gave us a room for the course. The women there also moved heaven and earth to find us crèche space and they put us on to Greenwich Toy Library who lent us crèche equipment. Camden Adult Education Institute was paying Clare for her work in Kentish Town. Kathryn asked our local Institute, Thameside, to do the same. Elaine and Lyn, the two outreach workers, were enthusiastic. They agreed to pay Clare as tutor/co-ordinator, and Iris, one of the GAGOU Women's Group, to teach Maths. But they could not afford to pay for the crèche or for the free lunches, which we had decided might be critical in deciding whether women could come or not, given that bus fares were so high.

We decided to fund-raise. Our best idea was illegal. The time co-incided with the People's March for Jobs reaching Greenwich. We thought we'd hold a raffle at the rally – but we weren't allowed to because of something to do with the Lotteries Act. So we asked for donations starting with GAGOU, who gave us £10.00 – their entire capital. Simba, a black people's project in the borough, the Community Development team, the Equal Opportunities Commission and War on Want all donated.

One of the interesting things about the GAGOU Women's Group by this time was that the process of planning all of this opened up possibilities for some of the members, which meant that attending a course was no longer a priority. We had found some of the 'knowledge' and confidence we had been looking for in working together and creating the course. But we wanted to open things up for other women who had not been able to be involved in the planning. We publicised the course in different ways. We produced a short leaflet, took it to school gates, launderettes, local shops, our front windows, neighbourhood centres, bus-stops, housing estates, the parks, the People's March for Jobs rally. The local press took it up there and wrote an article called 'Homework-break for the Girls'. Somehow the leaflets got fly posted – we don't know who did that – but mainly we talked.

Fifteen women came to the introduction, two from our original group (plus Iris teaching the Maths) and thirteen completed it. The age range was 20 to 55 years. We got in most of our original syllabus – except for the trade unions; the new group was not too bothered about them and we had gone off the idea too. Unions seem a bit removed if you don't have work. We found that as it was mostly new women who didn't know each other who attended, so a lot of space had to be given to getting to know one another, sharing about our lives and confidences, building the kind of communication that some of us had initially gone through as part of the Women's Group. More time was needed than we had planned, for some women to have individual space with Clare, and either Elaine or Lyn from the Institute were there most of the time for back-up. It was mid-summer when the course finished and some of the women came together in the autumn and tried to start something called the 'Old and Young, Fat and Thin Drama Group'. This never really got off the ground. Some women were busy with full-time commitments by this time and GAGOU was involved with other things. The hours and hours of women power that went into the setting-up and back-up of the original course could not be summoned up again. So much had happened outside the actual course – weekends spent planning over tuna salad, compiling funding applications, collectively writing Pat's curriculum vitae over the whole of one night – and so on – that we were all exhausted.

We are not sure if we can formally evaluate the process we have been discussing. We are clear though that any measure of what went on has to include more than how many women went on to which 'O' levels and jobs, important though these personal achievements are in themselves. There are a lot of unresolved issues. The Women's Planning Group of GAGOU decided that they wanted something to change in their lives and the lives of other women. Having got to this point, they contacted women who were waged to work and teach in the field of women 'returners'. Though the Women's Group decided on their own curriculum they certainly utilised an educational model that was influenced by the constraints of a learning establishment: for example, even if the group had wished to continue for longer, the length was prescribed by the length of the summer term and there was the prospect of fees (though most of these were waived). The course was held in a semi-public place, a community centre, unlike the planning which went on in people's front rooms. We can't tell how much these factors influenced what went on, but it was mainly new women who had been contacted by the GAGOU publicity who responded, not the original Women's Group, who by the time it started had moved on to other things. We know that the process of working together started ripples, sowed seeds and changed attitudes, not just for ourselves but for many of the agencies and organisations that had been involved. Each woman who was involved had a personal view of what a 'new opportunity' was for her. For some, particularly the older women, it was the opportunity to break isolation, for some the opportunity to get into further education.

There was certainly a feeling of excitement for us over this period which we have decided was to do not only with women working together but with women having the unusual experience of getting what they wanted. And though the whole political and economic climate is even bleaker now for women than it was in 1981, when Pat meets some of the course members in the supermarket they still talk about how their lives were changed.

19 'The Changing Experience of Women' at the Open University
Diana Leonard

For an institution which prides itself on innovation, both in the content of its courses and its style of teaching, the Open University (OU) has been rather late on the scene with a women's studies course. First appearing in January 1983, and scheduled to run for the next six years, the course whose production I have been involved with since 1980 comes ten years behind the first women's studies courses in Britain and more than a dozen years behind those in the USA.

That it came about at all was, as usual in women's studies, the result of pressure from below. However, the absence of students from the central campus at Milton Keynes, where courses are written and the national network of regional offices co-ordinated, meant that students did not play their usual role in demanding a course be put on. Instead it was pressure from a women's group involving administrative staff and lecturers, and support from outside the university, which first set the ball rolling. A small group of non-lecturer staff (including one man) continued to press the proposal through all the steps necessary to get it accepted and funded. These people worked in their own time, on top of their regular jobs within the OU; and when they needed to call in outsiders for advice, and eventually a consultant to write a formal proposal and draft of the first unit of the course, they got funds from UNESCO. The usual faculty backing for new courses – staffing and funding and the political support of those in high places – was largely missing, and more material was required by the committees than is usual at approval stage. Indeed, throughout the process of course production, we constantly were required to justify ourselves to the authorities more than is usual, although in the end they accepted our decisions.

The steering group chose to try to get the course accepted as part of the U (for University)-Area. This is a sector of the university distinct from the six faculties, though drawing staff in temporarily from any faculty. For administrative purposes each course within the U-Area is located in one faculty – ours is in Science. The U-Area was set up to encourage multi-disciplinary courses 'dealing with subjects of general interest . . . often closely related to everyday experience, questions and issues' in new areas of study (Guide to the Associate Student Programme 1983). All U-Area courses are available, and written so as to be accessible, to students with a foundation course in any faculty (Science, Maths, Technology, Arts, Social Science or Educational Studies). They can also be taken as separate courses by people (Associate Students) who are not taking a BA with the OU. This clearly provides an ideal location for women's studies – as has the occasional centre for interdisciplinary work in other institutions.

Being inter-faculty has certainly had beneficial influences on our course. It has encouraged us not to spend valuable time critiquing the disciplines (in which I confess I was at first one of the worst offenders), but rather to draw from them material of use to women in understanding their past and present situation. Although some may still see the course as overly sociological (partly because sociology has been the discipline in the UK in which feminism has had most impact and where much work has been done, and partly because some of the central course team members have been sociologists), we have consciously given space not only to literature, history and biology, but also economics, media studies, law and technology.

However (and there is always a 'however'), it was only possible to get half a credit for a new course within the U-Area at the time our course was approved. This means that students can take women's studies as only 1/12 of the work for their degree, and the course cannot require more than eight hours work a week for the thirty-two weeks of our academic year. This is not a lot, and it has to cover not only time for studying the main correspondence texts, but also reading articles in the reader, watching the TV programmes, listening to audio-cassettes (and reading the notes and exercises associated with the last two items), and some at least of the work involved in doing the four assignments (which are part of the formal assessment). And half-credit courses are less popular with students because they know that taking two half-credit courses is more work than taking one full-credit.

A second drawback to being in the U-Area is that it is a very fluid and unprotected sector of the university. Being part of it meant endless staffing problems and having one's associates scattered in offices all over the campus, each one subjected to conflicting demands from their 'home' discipline, and with little possibility of informal discussions to sort out problems or cement social relations. In addition, the U-Area does not have a dean or a faculty board or any power base within the university. When the education cuts started to bite, this was the sector the hierarchy first selected for the axe, though it has since been reprieved. It will need a fight to keep and to remake the women's studies course at the end of its present run.

The OU is organised quite democratically and it is open to any one on the staff to participate in the team that gets together to produce a particular course, provided they can justify the work they do each year to their superior. However, few who had initially put themselves forward to join the women's studies course had had much past involvement with women's studies. As often happens, many people wanted to work on the course in order to learn about the subject; while the fact that so few already qualified people were present within the OU reflects past staffing priorities and what disciplines have been seen as important areas. No one available to chair the course team satisfied the university authorities. The latter were somewhat nervous of feminism, and the terms of the acceptance of the course proposal by the Courses Committee and the Pro Vice-Chancellor (Academic) was that two people with 'solid qualifications in the area and as much seniority as possible' be seconded in from other universities to work on it.

Two of us duly arrived, initially for two years, in 1980, and set to work with a group which usually involved about eight other academics (though over the years sixteen different individuals were involved). These included a course manager, two people from IET (Institute of Educational Technology) and two staff tutors from regional offices who advised us on teaching style (including whether the drafts of the correspondence texts were sufficiently 'student active', as opposed to authors just talking at the students, and the form our assignments should take), as well as lecturers. The course team also included four people from the BBC, two editors, one designer, three secretaries and a librarian who helped us find pictures and cartoons to illustrate the units. We contracted a dozen external consultants to write either course units or modules for the summer school, and fourteen external assessors and an overall course assessor to be sent material for comments and academic approval at various stages. We have produced 16 units of correspondence material divided in 13 books, a 400-page reader, 11 TV programmes and a week-long programme for a summer school. Currently 30 local part-time tutors are involved in meeting our first 750 students from all over the UK and marking their essays. It has been, in short, a massive undertaking. (On top of which five babies were produced by members of the course team!)

We felt conscious, as we worked, of the importance of this course as constituting a visible acceptance of women's studies as a subject area, and of the richness of the resources we had at our disposal. Yet, faced with the wealth of material which currently exists on women, we had to make some tough decisions on what to include and what to leave out, so as to ensure we didn't overload the students: that they could do what they were set in the time available, and that whatever was included was used to the full. This was good discipline for me personally. It is all too easy to

draw up extravagantly long reading lists for courses, or to let
students buy books which are subsequently little used, as if because
they have the list in front of them one has 'covered the field', and if
they don't read the book now, well, they will at some time in the
future.

Because we had what seemed at the start like a lot of time in
which to prepare the course, we spent a great deal of time initially
discussing and rediscussing the overall structure of the course –
where to start from, where to end up, what order to go through in
between, what to have separate units on, and who should write
what – while at the end important decisions were made, at speed,
by a small number of people working flat out. Some of the initial
discussions were productive; many were not. We went round in
circles and sisterhood was thin on the ground. There is no perfect
order, no universally acceptable balance of perspectives, and
although there were important points at issue, there were also
times when individual interest got confused with political and
academic principle. Measured debate and consciousness-raising fit
ill with the exigencies of course production.

Despite our self-consciousness, U221, *The Changing Experience of
Women* is, of course, not *the* definitive women's studies course, even
for Britain in 1983. It is a construct in its own right, the product of
the membership and interaction of a particular course team which
is itself a coalition and not a consensus. It represents the
interweaving of *our* ideas and concerns, which are the result of our
various biographies, including our disciplinary training, research
experience and political involvements. But it is a construct with
which the course team can, I think, be pleased. It does contain a
range of interesting and important material and does cover most
areas developed in this country in the last decade. There is no
single perspective (other than a generalised 'feminism') pervading
the course, but rather a number of different viewpoints are put
forward by different authors (including some they themselves do
not share.) We tried to make as clear as possible to students the
reasons which lead people to differences of interpretation, explanation and practical politics and to indicate the disagreements within
the course team. The OU is much concerned, rightly, that its
courses avoid 'leading students'.

I am less certain we managed to avoid the counterside of this:
something which has always worried me about OU course units –
rather bland homogenised taste, with the loose ends tied up. It is
all too easy to maintain 'academic distance' from individual

experience and to downplay political difference by leaving out really contentious areas. Women's studies can be exciting precisely because there is a sense of ideas being raw, newly developed, by flesh and blood individuals and groups, arguing about meaningful differences of practice and analysis, which is open for students themselves to move forward, where they can make original contributions. This can be lost in the circumstances where a neat and tidy 'balanced' package of printed material plops through your letterbox and you read it in isolation.

As members of a distance-teaching institution, the opportunities for women Open University students to get together informally for support or CR is limited to 'self-help' groups they may organise for themselves – or external involvement in the women's liberation movement. There are only seven hours of tutorial contact time budgeted per student, and the students may be scattered over wide areas in some parts of the country. Tutor-led groups meet in a few study centres in each region and too infrequently to build up trust; only about a third of students are able (or want) to attend them; and they are quite properly taken up with academic problems and discussion. Some are mixed, since (in the first year of presentation of the course) 7 per cent of the students are men. (I hope more men will enrol in future, since a correspondence course seems an ideal way for interested men to listen and learn about women's experience.) It does mean, however, that our students may have to deal with the changes involved in becoming a feminist – the sense of becoming increasingly oppressed (or increasingly feeling an oppressor) as one becomes increasingly aware, and increasingly uncertain how to interpret everyday solutions and interactions – on their own. They lack the solidarity, warmth and joy which can characterise women's studies at its best.

Because of this, we decided that it was essential our course include a summer school, although it was not an easy decision to reach for several reasons: because it greatly increases its cost (the course itself cost an associate student £195 and the summer school an extra £120; because quite a lot of students are put off a half-credit course with a summer school; and because there were enormous difficulties in providing half-way adequate childcare. However, after the first year's experience of running the one-week course four times at the University of East Anglia, I am certain we made the right choice. It was a very positive experience for all who participated – whether as students, tutors or other members of staff.

One of our concerns in relation to summer school was to make it possible for women to be in single-sex groups if they wanted to be. This had to be done officially – we could not let it 'fall to chance' as in other women's studies courses. This suggestion was rceived very unfavourably within the OU. It was questioned in detail at the first committee to which we applied and then when it was finally agreed and our proposal went through to a higher committee, which could have been expected simply to approve it, it was stopped and we had to come and defend ourselves. It was suggested men could not be expected to talk about sexuality (one of our modules) without women present, or even that there was no precedent for single-sex education! The compromise we reached was to make differences of interaction in mixed and women-only groups the subject of discussion at summer school. In the first year we had an initial session raising the issue and then left women free to choose at the start of each of the three day-and-half long modules whether they wanted to be with people of the same or mixed sex. This didn't work very well. Some students found it forced a choice upon them, others felt it was unfair to men (if men were students on the course, they should not be discriminated against). It also meant that the women with the most experience of the women's liberation movement all opted for the women-only groups, leaving some of the other groups without a feminist student presence to enliven the discussion.

In 1984 we plan to have single-sex tutor (not teaching) groups, which will meet throughout the week and discuss what students want from the course, how they are progressing, and their individual problems, as well as reflecting on differences of interaction in different sorts of groups. We hope this will allow men students also time to discuss their particular concerns – e.g. many of them were given a fair bit of aggression by men on the other courses running alongside ours on the campus.

As a multi-disciplinary women's studies course we have, as I said, spent little time or space criticising the biases or gaps in sociology, economics, biology, etc. Those working on producing the course have now returned to their various departments, leaving only two workers to maintain it, as is usual in the OU. Feminism is currently little in evidence in existing Open University courses, and how well former U221 course team workers and other feminists on the OU staff will fare in trying to improve this in future remains to be seen. Attempts have already been made to suggest particular topics need not be included in the remake of certain courses, because 'they are dealt with in the women's studies course' – but the proposals have been squashed. There is certainly no sign of a positive push to make permanent appointments of specialists in this area – and the important impetus of day-to-day pressure from students on individual staff members to give support is missing. The fight will be uphill. On the other hand, the atmosphere towards women's studies *has* changed. Many people on campus expected the two of us who came in especially to work on the course to be sensational individuals, and the course units to be extreme and raving. But we were normal, and the course is now seen as 'having an important point to make' – even if it is not one the University establishment intends to prioritise, or even to protect when making cuts.

We can only hope *The Changing Experience of Women* continues to attract a lot of students, and that they are vociferous in their enthusiasm! But of course, the package we are offering *is* expensive, and when women are financially dependent it may not be an area their husbands are particularly willing to pay for. On the other hand, the books making up the course are in bookshops (from 1984) and can be borrowed from local libraries, and the television programmes are not on at too ungodly an hour (this year at least). We know that our reader was appreciated, since it sold out within a month of publication and had to be reprinted (as did a pamphlet by Michelle Stanworth, read in conjunction with the unit on women and girls' education), something which has never happened to an Open University set book before.

Part III

Chapter 4
What sort of Education? What sort of Culture?

The educational experiences and innovations described in the case studies give some idea of the enormous, but hidden, variety of learning taking place among women in Britain. The difficulties they have highlighted should make those who work in adult education more aware of the obstructions and cautions of bureaucratic structures and financing, as well as drawing attention to the dangers of complacent presumptions about women's needs. They have broken or at least cracked the mould of some traditional assumptions and provision, and turned to new kinds of educational proceses.

The first group, entitled 'Access' shows that without adequate literacy, language and basic education skills as well as thorough and effective educational counselling and guidance, the concept of continuing education, 'second chance for women', call it what you will, is a dead letter and mere rhetoric from those who hold the purse strings. The second group, loosely called 'Courses', attempts to highlight areas where existing traditional institutions and structures have been used by professionals working within them to provide new opportunities for women. The third group, defined by the phrase 'Extending the subject', includes case studies that show how women who are generally outside institutions, but not always, have used these to extend the scope and range of traditional women's subjects, e.g. the Sheffield Clothing Co-operative and the courses and training for childminders. There are also examples of how traditional male subjects are being made available to women, e.g. the New Technology courses at Liverpool and the work that is being done by the Deptford Skills Centre. The fourth group on 'Women in Centres' highlighted some of the strengths, frustrations and successes of women when they have organised together around the general idea of providing a voice, a space and a subject for women. The Totnes Women's Centre is particularly interesting in showing what can be achieved by women together without any formal funding. Sometimes women have used the system; sometimes they haven't. It has almost always been a struggle. In the final section, 'Processes', the case studies show how women have often had to struggle against the hierarchies, beg for money and justify their demands, not always successfully, in an attempt to make the existing structures more relevant to the educational needs of women. These show that sometimes the processes of working together as women have been more important than the end product, if there is one. Centres move from group to group, subjects and needs change from one class to the next, but the process is not set. It is concerned with growth, both individually and collectively, and with change.

Nevertheless it is apparent that most education for adult women is based on and conditioned by traditional assumptions of social, sexual, family and economic roles. The 'front-end' model of education, where people learn and store up large chunks of knowledge in compulsory schooling from 5 to 16 years, is at variance with our concept that the fragmentation of women's lives can and should be used as a positive educational model for women and by extension for everyone. Such a model relates quite easily to the philosophy behind continuing education for adults. This emphasises and expects that people will opt in and out of education throughout their lives as they want or as they need it. This breaking down of education into smaller and more manageable parts would seem to have benefits for women and men rather than the present inflexible and divisive pattern of education identified in the front-end model, but also echoed to a large extent in our system of further and higher education. Although adult education does not easily fit the formal educational model and this is one of its strengths, it is also conditioned and organised to bolster existing assumptions about cultural and social patterns – men and work, women and family, immigrant comunities and basic education, unskilled men and women (working class) and literacy.

Mee and Wiltshire in their informative study of Local Education Authority adult provision, *Structure and Performance in Adult Education* (1978) found that although in theory there was freedom to provide and teach, three-quarters of the 22,761 courses they examined were basically similar. In other words there is a large common core curriculum in local education authority education for adults in spite of the fact that there is, in theory, the freedom to innovate

and there are no officially imposed syllabuses or examinations
(Mee and Wiltshire: 1978: 41). Their research shows that the
curriculum can be divided into the following categories:

		%
1	*Craft and aesthetic skills*	
	(i) Courses related mainly to personal care and household economy	33.6
	(ii) Courses related mainly to leisure time enjoyment	19.5
2	*Physical skills*	
	(i) Courses related mainly to health and fitness	9.3
	(ii) Courses related mainly to leisure time enjoyment	14.8
3	*Intellectual and cognitive skills*	
	(i) Language courses	10.9
	(ii) Other courses	5.8
		16.7
4	*Courses for disadvantaged groups*[1]	6.1

(For a more detailed breakdown of courses and
subjects see Appendix 'C': 124-5 in Mee and Wiltshire.)

The largest type of provision, one-third, is concerned mainly
with the traditional female domestic arts and crafts, beauty culture,
car maintenance, cookery, dress-making, flower arrangement,
gardening, soft-furnishing. This kind of provision is also the staple
diet of the Townswomen's Guilds, the Women's Institutes and
other voluntary women's organisations (see Appendix). The
findings of the 1982 Advisory Council for Adult & Continuing
Education (ACACE) Report on *Adults: Their Educational Experience
and Needs*, where people were asked what subjects they would like
to learn about which they had not previously studied seems to
confirm this tendency for the traditional basic subjects with women
and men opting for the stereotypic female and male subjects
(ACACE: 1982: 73, Table 7.7).

33% of the women and only 2% of the men said they would like to study domestic science. On the other hand 18% of the men and only 6% of the women asked for carpentry and do-it-yourself classes compared to 16% of the women and only 11% of the men who said they would like to study creative subjects (art, painting, sculpture and pottery). In relation to what people already studied where more women than men participate in general cultural and creative subject areas the report commented as follows, 'We do not know, however, whether this genuinely relates to differences in interest or temperament between men and women, or whether men *simply do not have the time* because of the more pressing need for work related courses' (our italics) (ACACE: 1982: 55). It is ironic that the writers of this report should so overtly imply that it is more necessary for men than for women to take work-related courses when we know that men already have more professional qualifications than women. It is interesting to observe that foreign languages and domestic science were the first two options listed in the question which asked people what they would like to study (ACACE: 1982: 124, Question 18); 53% of the women ticked these as their first choices compared with 25% of the men. What might have been the results *if* the question had been ordered differently and different options suggested which were opening up other areas of study? For example, astrology, black studies/race relations, environmental subjects, health, parenthood, psychology, women's studies?

From these results policy-makers and providers of classes for adults could be confirmed in their argument that what's on offer is largely what is wanted, judged by the student take-up and by the potential study choices of other adults. This claim is analogous to the supermarket versus the corner shop debate. Customers – and students are customers in the existing models of adult education – pick out the goods which appear on the shelves rather than ask for brands they cannot see or may well prefer to buy. In contrast the corner shop is closer to the community education centre model whose local users and shoppers can more comfortably and immediately discuss and express their demands and choices. Ideally discussion and choice should be part of every centre providing adult education. Women have been so conditioned by the primacy of their family roles that, caught in a sort of double-bind, they feel they must take the domestic subjects in which they already have knowledge and experience, and also because if they are spending household money (their wages) on themselves, they would feel guilty if they wasted it on something seeming not so useful. Besides they may, as yet, only be half aware of what they might want to study. It is interesting that women students who have been on Return-to-Study, Second Chance, Fresh Horizon courses become more articulate about what they need (see Hutchinson: 1978; Lee Centre: 1983; and Lovell: 1980). Bridget Barber, in a survey of Crowborough in Sussex found that many women attending daytime classes felt they should really have been at home at work whilst their husbands were out at work (Barber: 1980: 48). Some confirmation of this as yet relatively unexplored area is revealed in a recently survey amongst the audience of the South of England based television station TVS. This found that only 8-10 per cent of women at home in the afternoon watched television. One respondent said, 'It's a working day', and another 'I feel I should be contributing in a *working* way' (Angela Lambert: *Sunday Times*: 30.10.83).

Bias and control

So often assumptions or expectations of what people, and particularly women, are capable of are belied by what they do, or prove to want. For so long educators have thought that women were congenitally unable to understand mathematics and were uninterested in scientific subjects, and this bias has accordingly been built into the design of class programmes and research.

The BBC assumed that its computer literacy project would be more relevant to men than women and so weighted its test sample significantly towards them – 69% compared with 35% women (BBC: 1981: 90). However the audience for the Monday night programmes was made up of 47% women and 53% men which seems to be a remarkably high figure given the assumed lack of interest women have in technology, there was a 'slight over representation of men' said the BBC (BBC: 1983: 1). No breakdown of viewers by sex was given for the Sunday morning and Monday afternoon programmes but it is possible that if these figures had been included more women than men would actually have seen the programmes.

People continue to have the strong belief that computing is still really a man's field. When questioned about whether the presenters were right for the series, 86% and 84%, respectively, of the sample felt the two men were right, but only 62% voted for the female presenter (BBC: 1983: 28). A sexist ambiguity appears to exist in the public mind which is more reluctant to accept women presenters being in charge of disseminating knowledge which, after all, is a form of power. Will adult educators respond to the implications of these findings or will they continue to assume that computer studies are mainly a 'male' subject and therefore frame the publicity and the class programmes in a language which is alienating to women. The objective of one computer course at a further education college in Scotland was publicised as follows:

> To make available to people the opportunity to become either acquainted with computers on an appreciation level, or develop skills in order to make decisions from a position of informed knowledge about computers and computing. (Gartside: 1982: 3)

According to the 1982 Advisory Council for Adult and Continuing Education Report, 6% of men and only 1% of women had taken courses in computer studies (ACACE: 1982: 54).

The conclusions that researchers or organisers draw from factual evidence may differ from the perceptions of women. In a survey of extra-mural students in the Liverpool area in 1978/9, the majority of the women (76) described themselves as retired and only 58 as housewives. The writer suggests that 'one may safely assume that many of them (the women) left their jobs to become housewives and might well have been classified under that heading instead' (*The Tutors' Bulletin*: Spring 1981: 16). Ironically the women obviously answered the question in the way they thought they were expected to; they used age (i.e. their retirement from paid work) as an indicator when they, more than anybody else, must have been aware that women never retire from housewifery.

Research, although it is believed to be unbiased and accepted as such, is still permeated by traditional assumptions about male and female roles, and tends to frame the questions in terms of the results it wishes or expects to obtain (see Helen Roberts: 1981; Liz Stanley and Sue Wise: 1983). As Jean Baker Miller has so acutely pointed out:

> A dominant group, inevitably, has the greatest influence in determining a culture's overall outlook – its philosophy, morality, social theory, and even its science. The dominant group, thus, legitimises the unequal relationship and incorporates it into society's guiding concepts. The social outlook, then, obscures the true nature of this relationship – that is, the very existence of inequality. The culture explains the events that take place in terms of other premises, premises that are inevitably false, such as racial or sexual inferiority. . . .

Inevitably the dominant group is the model for 'normal human relationships'. It then becomes 'normal' to treat others destructively and to derogate them, to obscure the truth of what you are doing, by creating false explanations, and to oppose actions towards equality. In short, if one's identification is with the dominant group, it is 'normal' to continue in this pattern. (Baker Miller: 1976: 8)

She goes on to say:

Dominants are usually convinced that the way things are is right and good, not only for them but especially for the subordinates. (9)

This analysis of dominants and subordinates is mirrored within the male-controlled adult education system. Opening up more provision for women at all levels of educational need is not sufficient. Just more of the same or greater access to existing provision does not mean true equality, since fitting into or expanding upon what is already provided changes neither the structure, the ideology nor women's position in the wider society.

Hilary Friend points this out in a comment on another ACACE document (*Continuing Education: From Policies to Practice*, 1980): 'Continuing Education cannot imagine women having any needs other than the need to be in the system' (Friend: 1982: 12). Some of the case studies (see in particular Nos 15, 16 and 19) show the institutional and emotional reactions to innovations proposed and taken by women in their attempts to work out new kinds of education better suited to their needs. Education should not be only about safety first. It is also about jumping into the pool and learning not only to survive but to swim.

Not only are the subjects people study influenced by certain kinds of bias but there is the whole area of what educators term 'the hidden curriculum'. Elizabeth Vallance defines this usefully as:

the inculcation of values, political socialisation, training in obedience and docility, the perpetuation of the class structure. . . . I use the term to refer to those non-academic but educationally significant consequences of schooling that occur systematically but are not made explicit at any level to the public rationales for education. (quoted by Deem: 1978: 47)

Although she is arguing here about sexism in the school system, her definition is also applicable to adult education. For example there are the obvious barriers which prevent easy access to education for women at different stages in their lives. These include: the question of fees – women's fees are often determined

by their relationship to a man, whether their husbands work or
not; the time and place of the class; the lack of childcare facilities;
the bureaucratic formalities of the system, the inflexibility of the
timetable (six/ten/twelve/twenty-four weeks and two hours per
week, with little holiday and weekend provision); registers; the cost
of materials; the language of the prospectus. Furthermore there is
the lack of adequate funding: old schools as centres, odd meeting
places and small spaces; little welcoming comforts, style and social
facilities. This is not entirely the fault of adult educators, who
manage on a shoe-string which keeps getting broken and has to be
re-knotted, but nevertheless there are ways in which things can be
rethought and reordered. Case Study No. 8 shows how an adult
education class in Sheffield built upon women's existing knowledge
and skills in making clothes to turn them into a potentially viable
form of paid employment. The Greenwich New Opportunities for
Women course (Case Study No. 18) describes how women together
valued and used their own experiences to devise a course which
was pertinent to themselves and their needs. They then asked an
adult education institute to provide the resources to make this
possible. Both these initiatives are individual instances of new
kinds of educational work, but did not continue because they were
isolated examples lacking the financial and institutional support of
a wider network.

In other cases prejudiced attitudes and power have been used as
a means of social control – the dominant over the subordinate, men
over women – in ways that hinder change. The following brief
examples are known to us and illustrate how this may happen in
practice.

1   *Making special allowances for men – women servicing men*
Looking through the prospectus of cookery classes at my local
Evening Institute, I noted with amusement that for all classes one
had to bring along one's own ingredients, except for the one entitled
'Mainly for Men Cookery' – for this all ingredients are provided by
the tutor. Men may learn to cook, but of course they are far too busy
(unlike working wives) to do the shopping too. (Margaret Drabble
in *Half the Sky*: 1979: 68)

2   *Meaning to be helpful but seeing women as deficient*
A course in an outer London borough was entitled: Car Maintenance for Ladies of little Ability. (1983).

3   *Controlling resources*
The women's section of the Labour party in a working-class East

London constituency planned a residential weekend course in an adult education centre away from the family; but they arranged that if necessary fathers and children could camp nearby. They were aware that other weekend courses had been subsidised by the constituency party in the past. When they asked for funding they were refused. So they were forced to raise money in the typical women's way of jumble sales and raffles in order to ensure that all the women who wanted to come on the course could do so (1979).

4 *Controlling the curriculum*

A Manpower Services Commission (MSC) funded a 'Wider Opportunities for Women' (WOW) course in an Inner London Education Authority adult education institute was visited by an Inner London Education Authority Inspector who said that what the women needed was more English and Maths. Looking around at the three women staff, he remarked that they might need to know about their maternity rights under the Employment Protection Act (1975), but this was not at all relevant to the students (1980).

5 *Fear of losing control*

A part-time women adult educator in a rural local education authority centre found her plans for a women's education day constantly being undermined and derided by her principal. At one point he suggested that she would do well to have male observers on the day. And when he reported on the proposed education day to the governors he described it as a study conference for females only and that they were keeping it a secret (1983).

6 *Making women's issues invisible*

The programme for a recent national conference for home economics lecturers in further and higher education included conference objectives relating to equal opportunities in terms of race and gender. During one evening of the course, members were allowed a choice of activities, one of which was a discussion on equal opportunities. There was an overwhelming response from both women and men and clearly the issues discussed were seen as highly relevant to the future development of this specialist area. In the summing-up of an otherwise important and worthwhile conference, little reference was made to what had emerged in the discussions as a major conference issue (1983).

7 *Not letting go*

At the launch of the Workers' Educational Association's Women's Studies Teaching Pack the session was chaired by the new male district secretary of the region where the pack had been researched and developed. He was surrounded by three women who had actually done the work, and with his female predecessor, who had started the project, sitting in the audience (1983).

These illustrations may seem minor and petty but added together and continuously applied they have the cumulative effect of neglecting women and limiting their educational opportunities.

Even the so-called 'trivialities' as to how women are named are indicative of how they are perceived and indeed trivialised.[2] The arguments over the use of 'Mrs' and 'Ms' is well known. But in adult education there are some funny anomalies. In prospectuses it is common to see women tutors as Mrs/Miss M. Block compared with I. Block, even E. Block, Esq. The illogicalities of ladies keep fit and women's weight training – there are never gentlemen in adult education; hostess cookery (cookery for hosts? liberating cookery?); dressmaking (making clothes?); the jokes about women's studies – why not men's studies? Why not indeed if only men would start them?[3] There are many kinds of subtle, even seemingly unimportant ways, in which 'the dominant group usually holds all of the open power and authority and determines the way in which power may be acceptably used' (Baker Miller: 1978: 9).

Culture

We are arguing that in effect our culture and education is 'man-made'. The production of knowledge and therefore the making of culture – art, literature, politics, science – is determined by those who make it, order it, interpret it and dispense it. It is claimed and believed that this is an asexual, objective and universal process. But in truth women have not played a major part in producing the concepts and cultural forms which are the backbone of our society. Dorothy Smith in her important essay, 'A Peculiar Eclipsing: Women's Exclusion from Man's Culture', argues that

> our experience has not been represented in the making of our culture. There is a *gap* between where we are and the means we have to express and act. It means that the concerns, interests, experiences forming 'our' culture are those of men in positions of dominance whose perspectives are built on the silence of women (and of others). (Smith: 1978: 282)

She extends and enlarges upon the premise with particular reference to education and the role it plays in society:

The exclusion of women from participating in creating the culture of the society is in this day and age largely organised by the ordinary social processes of socialisation, education, work and communication. These perform a routine, generalised, and effective repression. The educational system is an important aspect of this. It trains people in skills they need to participate at various levels in the ideological structuring of the society (they must be able to read at least); it teaches them the ideas, the vocabularies, images, beliefs; it trains them to recognise and approve ideological sources (what kind of books, newspapers, etc. to credit, what to discredit, who are the authoritive writers or speakers and who are not). It is part of the system which distributes ideas and ensures the dissemination of new ideological forms as these are produced by the intelligentsia. It is also active itself in producing ideology, both in forms of critical ideas and theories in philosophy and literature. (Smith: 1978: 287-7)

Diana Leonard points out, as is obvious yet unrecognised, that women form the majority working in the institutions which produce knowledge as secretaries, technicians, assistants, part-time tutors, researchers and administrators. This list does not include the women and wives at home who service the policy-makers and the researchers as the creators of ideas and ideologies. Indeed without the nurturing and mothering given by women, men would not be freed to create new forms of knowledge, make new discoveries in science or construct new ways of ordering the world. So women *help* to make the cultural experience of our world and even to research 'women's experience' in it as part of this. But the truth is that it is *men's view* of human and consequently of women's experiences (see Leonard: 1983: 7).

In this subsidiary and supportive role women obviously lack authority as makers, purveyors and interpreters of culture, ideas and knowledge unless they have been granted special permission to assume such authority and be recognised as an expert or a specialist. According to the Equal Opportunities Commission, in 1979 only 4% of Cabinet Ministers were women, 3% of High Court Judges, 1% of University Professors and, as Eileen Byrne has pointed out only 3% of the government of education is by women (Byrne: 1978: 15). Furthermore women form only 23% of the membership of public bodies in Britain. Out of 874 public bodies 304 had no women members and 159 had only one woman (Hansard: 30 June 1982: 1017). Only 3% of Members of Parliament are women, a lower representation than in any West European parliament. And when they are there, not all women in high places 'generally present women's perspectives – even if they are appointed as token women. They are certainly not selected *by* other women *to* represent them' (Leonard: 1983: 6).

Women have been alienated from so many aspects of culture and the ways in which it is ordered. 'We have learned to live inside a discourse which is not ours and which expresses and describes a landscape in which we are alienated and which preserves that alienation as integral to its practice' (Smith: 1978: 294). In plain language Betty Friedan described this as the 'problem which has no name' (Friedan 1963: 17). The Greenham Common women have made visible non-violent resistence in their protest for peace. This may seem alienating and a novel way to men yet not to women. As one of the Greenham women said in a radio interview: 'In the past men left home to make war. Now women are leaving home to make peace.' In the organising of their strategies they have no leaders or hierarchies. They have relied on the unseen (i.e. non-public) networks of supportive women and women's groups, plus word of mouth, all over the country. When gathering to demonstrate, they and other women have made new rituals of public peaceful protest; they have decorated the perimeter fence of the Greenham air base with personal tokens and surrounded the base with thousands of women and children who have joined hands, sung songs and lighted candles. When they went to Parliament and were evicted from the public gallery, they quickly set up a children's corner in the main hall, and danced and sang with candles until the Members of Parliament went home. They themselves are not violent. What they have done is adopted some ideas from the Gandhian non-violent protest movement in India and the Campaign for Nuclear Disarmament Committee of One Hundred. In the process they have developed a social organisation of support unique to themselves. This is one example of ways in which women can make a culture and style of living that is their own. It is not the only model, but one among potential thousands.

There is a fair amount of research which points out the ways in which experts do not see, or hear, or notice what women feel and appreciate because women generally express themselves with diffidence or choose silence in order to retain a space for themselves (see among many others, Ehrenreich, Oakley, Olsen, Rich, Roberts, and Spender). Men as the specialists and deciders tend to label such doubts, queries and challenges to their knowledge and ways of doing – called logic – as deviant, atypical, immature, illogical, irrational and hence unfeminine.

The struggle to find a voice, and keep one, has led women, like other oppressed and suppressed groups – slaves, the working classes, Jews, lesbians and gays, the colonised, children – into creating their own subterranean culture and networks. Historically women have had unique ways of bonding together in cooking, farming, marketing, crafts and arts, health, childbearing, story-telling, singing, dancing and clowning. 'Women have always had distinctive art forms; journals and letters, lullabys and gossip and bedtime stories, quilts and embroidery, china-painting. As part of a woman's cultural movement, we have revived an interest in these forms, and look on them with a new respect' (Griffin 1982: 188). But having no overt power, especially not of the economic kind except through the family or kinship, women have had to be manipulative, often subversive, in order to create space and meaning for themselves and their children. Women should not have to gain recognition this way.

However there are some indications of change. Creative work by women is beginning to be recognised more publically, although this does not mean that it is yet fully accepted or tolerated. The great public interest in Judy Chicago's 'The Dinner Party' exhibition celebrates women's creativity (now in storage due to lack of financial support), whilst the Institute of Contemporary Arts (ICA) exhibition in 1980 of women painters' images of men began a process of shocking gallery-goers into new ways of seeing men as objects. The work of women film-makers, theatre groups and musicians, although still 'on the fringe', is beginning to dent the male monopolies of these art forms. The imaginative energy and volume of contemporary women's writing has made feminist ideas and experience more visible and caused a new interest in feminist literary criticism. But such developments could not have taken place without the backing of feminists publishers in Britain and the United States in recent years, and the fact that there is a receptive women's public to support this. Additionally there has been the spontaneous development of women's centres in many places as well as the free women's universities in Berlin and Rome. The controversial growth of women's studies, and issues around women's and girls' education, inside and outside the traditional universities, have shown up the problems of women's inequalities, but not yet changed awareness of how patriarchy permeates and penetrates all aspects of living. There is the newly developing sphere of oral history and the history workshop movement (as well as writers' and song workshops) which validate the formerly unknown personal life histories and experiences of women and men. *Mother Land*,[4] an account of black West Indian women's experiences of coming to Britain, researched, written and acted by their daughters, is an excellent example of how cultural perceptions can be extended. These are fragile growths which can be easily dissipated and disappear from view as has happened in the past to women's creations and cultures. (See among others, Mary Jacobus: 1978; Jill Liddington and Jill Norris: 1978; Tillie Olsen: 1980; Roszika Parker and Griselda Pollock: 1981; Elaine Showalter: 1978; Virginia Woolf: 1929: 1983.)

Any living society needs to be stimulated and enriched by mixing with and learning from other cultural experiences. The existence of separated cultures usually means that one has higher status than the others (middle class over working class, European over Afro-Caribbean, male over female). A multi-dimensional approach which is tolerant of the entire spectrum of others' realities would preserve individual cultures as well as creating new and enlarged kinds of cultural experiences (see also Stanley and Wise: 1983). However, as Caroline Bailey has observed, 'Oppressed and suppressed as many women undoubtedly are, it is still easier to get out from under the oppressor than it is to correct a distorted vision of the world' (Bailey: 1982: 5).

It is not a question of just inserting, or incorporating or tacking on the female perspective, but an *integrating* (to complete what is imperfect by the addition of the necessary parts: *The Shorter Oxford Dictionary* 1973) of women's perspectives and experiences. This will require a total re-vision of the world, both revising, rebuilding and re-seeing it in new ways (see Callaway: 1981: 34-43).

Notes

1 Since 1978 it is probable that courses for the so-called disadvantaged groups will have increased. For example in 1982 the Inner London Education Authority provided between 35 and 40% of its adult education for 'disadvantaged' groups (ILEA Inspector June 1983).

2 *Trivia*: another name of the goddess of hunting, Diana, because she presides over all places where three roads meet. Seeing her mother suffer in childbirth gave her an aversion to marriage, so her father, Jupiter, gave her permission to live in perpetual celibacy, and to care for the travails of women.

3 It is interesting that a decade after the introduction of women's studies in Britain there is now some movement towards men studying their roles and relationships in men's studies classes – we know of at least three

which have been started in 1983/4 in London. There have also been two television series on the subject of men: Channel 4 Autumn 1983 and BBC 2 January 1984. See also Phillip Hodson: 1984; Stuart Miller: 1983; Channel 4: About Men: 1983.

4 See Elyse Dodgson in *London Drama*, vol. 6, No. 7 Winter 1982: 10-13. And also the video-taped performance of *Motherland* made by the Inner London Education Authority.

Chapter 5
Dilemmas of Innovation

The dilemmas that concern us in this chapter are the difficult and complex problems surrounding the 'perspective transformation' of education for adults and for women in particular. It means educators and students asking the old questions in new ways and listening to the answers. The answers could be traditional, conventional, safe, new, radical, controversial, shocking, or extreme. It means being more aware of the multiplicity of demands, needs and choices that may be expressed. Institutions in particular, if they are to stand by their alleged educational philosophy of openness and democracy, will have to relinquish some power and control (i.e. resources) to the users and potential users in the community. It will not be sufficient to blur the issues by retreating behind the defences of the 'balanced programme' which can be accepted by all and forgotten by all. Neither will true equality be reached by selecting the token woman, the token black person or the token person with disabilities to share in the making of policy, sit on committees or be appointed to the staff. Nor is the two-hour-a-week crèche or the one class in women's/feminist studies enough. At such a level nothing will have really changed in the power relationships nor in the transformation of knowledge and the way it is studied. The notion of change, of openness, uncomfortable though it may be, has to be built into the education structure and programmes at all levels.

Let us analyse a familiar old question 'What do women want?' This is Freud's question, but it is also similar to the nineteenth-century debate labelled 'the woman question'. And we have all heard it in many ways, in many tones of voice and in many situations – at work, in the classroom, in the home, in the market-place, in pub and club, and in bed. It is always a question asked by men about women: and men provide the answers. The question is so defined that it is outside women who become 'the other', 'the deviant', the 'non-normal', 'the problem'. Women are seen as the object, but 'objectivity is the name we give to male subjectivity' (Spender, 1981: 5). The question is trying to fit women in, to accommodate them. And it is often answered – by men but not by most women – in benevolent, paternal (sometimes maternal) tones. We ask for freedom? 'Of course,' they say, 'but let us define the limits.' The unquestioned assumption is that what exists is human, best, just, rational and correct. But women in their present state do not define themselves and their wants in such terms. Neither do they reverse the question by asking what men want, since they already know what men want of them. The difficulty is when women connive and collude with the male view and expectations of them, thus fulfilling the cycle of interdependency – the oppressed upholding the oppressors.

Not all women would define the problem as we have just done. There is the dilemma that only a minority of women are feminists. Feminism and its exponents arouse fears of subversion and anarchy, the upturning of the existing 'natural' order. They are called 'unwomanly' because they are moving out of their given place. Indeed the public image of feminists and, therefore, women's studies as compared with women's subjects, challenges the conformity of the familiar and familial patterns of provision in education. The issue is over different versions of the world and what education should be about. This should not mean necessarily a separate world, but a world incorporating many separate strands of experience (multi-dimensional). Sandra Bartky describes it thus: 'Feminists are not aware of different things than other people: they are aware of the same things differently' (Bartky: 1977: 27, 33). By this she means feminist consciousness, which is not fixed, but one of evolutionary change and process varying from woman to woman (see Stanley and Wise: 1983: 123). By seeing things differently and perceiving the need to move from deconstruction of power relationships to a new reconstruction feminists come into conflict with those who hold the more traditional male-provided view. The issue is not greater equality and incorporation into the existing system, but its transformation. There is a lack of awareness, a lack of understanding, and an unwillingness to study the world in a different way, to allow for different states of consciousness and interpretation. Most people seem to be more comfortable with the discomforts and inequalities of the present – they prefer the devil/witch they know – rather than risk the uncertainties and disequilibrium of the unknown, of change. And yet education proclaims that it is about change?

Constraints

One of the main barriers to change is the fact that the formal part of adult education is too closely modelled upon full-time schooling for children and the higher education system, which are highly structured, timetabled, examination-conscious and institutionally authoritarian. It still has an image of being a freetime service which paradoxically tends to stop when people have the most leisure time – at weekends, in the holidays. In general only the Workers Educational Association (WEA) and universities provide weekend and summer schools which break this pattern to some extent. Yet even these may restrict the student membership because of the fees, the lack of childcare provision and the difficulty (for women) of being away from home. Unless there is universal childcare provision, as an integral part of education policy, women are being denied access to a large part of the class programme. It is also possible to censor what they are able to learn by limiting the choice of subjects in buildings where crèches are provided. For example, crèche provision on two mornings a week in a building where only literacy, English as a Second Language (ESL), pottery and dress-making are offered is restrictive.

Sometimes it even seems as though the service has forgotten its prime responsibility towards the adult population. Because of the government cuts and stop-go policies in recent years it has tended to take the comparatively simple bureaucratic decision of reducing the numbers of classes: for example, from 900 to 750 adult classes annually in the University of London; from 35 to 30 weeks a year in the ILEA or down to even 20 weeks in other LEAs. Such harsh reductions hold back innovation and experimentation and result in a defensive education service.

It is increasingly the case that for new initiatives, women are having to approach a variety of funding bodies because education authorities lack the money or the will to provide the support services that would mean genuine open access to women. Case Study No. 18 is a classic example of this dilemma. A community centre provided the room; the Toy Library lent crèche equipment; the Adult Education Institute paid the tutors; and 5 national and local organisations gave donations. The search for money requires a large amount of time, organisation and consultation. The end result, after so much effect, may be a once-only class or provision that fails to meet the original aims. A recent Adult Literacy & Basic Education Unit special project, which gave free literacy tuition to women on a council estate in East Anglia, is another example of how their expectations of education were raised, to be dashed when they wanted to move into mainstream classes for which they had to pay high fees.

But apart from these external monetary constraints there are other factors which make change difficult. Most women have minor positions in the education organisations and therefore little chance to influence policy-making (in a system, to repeat ourselves, where they are both the majority of students and teachers). Women part-time tutors perhaps feel diffident about rocking the boat with demands or criticisms, because next year's contract and pay packet rests almost entirely within the gift of the programme-planners (male). Women generally are not as experienced at negotiating with authority as their male counterparts, and, in addition, their position as part-time tutors may be their only job outside the domestic world, which gives them money and some status: male part-time tutors more usually have other full-time jobs from which they derive their financial and social standing.

Consequently processes of proposing and instigating change or new ideas are not easy. After all it is extremely difficult for women tutors (part-time and in the lower grades) to prove that a demand exists for new types of classes and that they will work: especially if feminist, they will be seen as potentially subversive. Junior staff are often accused of being irresponsible when they make demands and arguments for new kinds of classes and are told that they 'don't understand. There's no money left in the budget'. Power is used to control knowledge and information which is often doled out in a personal and piecemeal way but is not available, as of right, to all members of staff. Women can be accused of manipulating power on the personal request – and – favour level, but this is done by men as well. Often men in positions of authority manipulate women's need to be needed by a friendly sexual cameraderie that makes refusal difficult. They expect women to take on tasks where they themselves shirk the responsibility, asking secretaries (women) to close classes or cope with a demanding tutor; or asking women, whatever their status, to do the maintenance and servicing jobs which they themselves would not do – making sandwiches for governors' meetings, washing the cups, or coping with accidents and illness. It is worth noting that the bureaucratic procedures, which have evolved to keep administrators in control and the staff busy, with the obsession with rules, registers, returns, reports and statistics, seem irrelevant and alienating to adult students. This tends to make adult education a reactive rather than an assertive service where the bureaucratic tail is seen to be wagging the dog. There is a tendency to close ranks and maintain what has always been, whether it is effective or not, rather than challenge it and suggest alternatives for the future.

Of course it is not only the staff who need their consciousness raised; there is the incalculable difficulty of estimating student response to innovatory programmes, quite apart from involving them in the planning processes. Indeed it has been common for working-class women and groups within the women's liberation movement to educate each other informally. They do not look to nor ask adult education for this. Adult education, being essentially geared to perpetuating women's domestic and family roles, has been reluctant to tackle some of the realities of women's everyday lives such as legal rights, racism, abortion, divorce, single parenthood, lesbianism, the menopause, cancer, bereavement and so on.

Adult education, although potentially different from the rest of formal education, still largely believes in the concept of teacher-taught, expert-novice, master-apprentice, and the handing down of good practices and pearls from the bank of cultural knowledge. This is not to deny the pleasure that people get from studying the classic texts, an imaginative novel or poem, great art or music, or debating philosophic ideas. But there is a circle of dependency created to which students have to constantly return to ask for reassurance, though this would be denied by tutors. How often is someone in a class for many years, still unable to grasp all the concepts, put the final touches to a garment, or is linked in cosy dependency on the tutor? In fact the expert tutor in the domestic crafts has colonised the knowledge and skills that women have always known, and, after professionalising them, returns them to women in a new educational package for which they have to pay. (See Ehrenreich & English: 1979: for their important work on the issue of male professionalism, and Keddie: 1981: unpublished paper: for relating it to adult education.) The women's liberation movement on the other hand, believes in the value of experience; that we are all experts or at least potentially so, who together develop and extend our true potential. It believes in a progression from the personal to the community and into the wider world.

Traditionally adult education has maintained a prescriptive and a political position within its general cultural and skills education programme. Both of these are used as mechanisms to decide and prescribe what should be available, on the seemingly rational grounds that order, continuity and variety are essential to an efficient adult education service which should provide a balanced curriculum. This, like a good home, provides food for everyone, be they carnivore, vegan or vegetarian. The education menu can be prescriptive, ameliorative, familiar and sometimes innovatory, but it is planned and ordered before the students come – in fact in order to attract the students (market-place model) – by a minority on the full-time staff. The labelling of groups as 'disadvantaged' (Russell: 1983: paras 277-85) is in itself an assumption and a prescription that both shows the unawareness of the provider-deciders towards groups of people who have developed their own ways of managing and surviving in their lives, relationships and work. Supposing the problems of provision had been looked at and tackled differently, as some of the case studies have shown to be possible. The question could then be asked: How can we learn from such groups?

Another control mechanism is not just neutralism towards and conformity with the prevailing ideology of society and of most people (middle-class, white, male, liberal-conservative?), but is defended – to the last desk – on the (in itself biased) argument that education for adults should be apolitical and as 'unbiased' as possible. Balance can lead to an infinite variety of provision or, it can, as is so often the case, lead to the lowest common denominator that uncritically attempts to be all things to all people at all times. It's rather like chicken as the main course at conference dinners; bland yet pleasant, and unlikely to offend many people's palates: the safe option. Surely it is now recognised that there is no such thing as bias-free scholarship and research, education and work practices, the media and the arts? One person's bias is another's balance. In an attempt to be balanced and fair, adult educators have slanted their provision towards the dominant national culture and specific female and male skills and qualities, thus bolstering the traditional and accepted family, work and class roles. They have generally been reluctant, if not covertly subversive, to the provision of childcare facilities for example, which would open classes to greater numbers of younger women. Is this because parenting and the care of children is seen as the mother's responsibility, hidden away in the home, the private domain? In the same way they have not encouraged women-only classes or separate provision for minority groups.

Intangibles

It is difficult to pinpoint the less visible barriers because of unspoken fears and prejudices. These are not always admitted or recognised. Where women are concerned men still are unwilling to accept us as autonomous responsible beings. We must stay as we are or else anarchy will break out and the 'rational order' will be overturned. In times of expansion educators seem able to adapt to challenge and change in moderate doses – probably because they know they can fall back on the entrenched control mechanisms of the institution – but when there is uncertainty over finances and jobs, they become even more defensive of their traditions and policies. In addition people stop listening because they get tired and resentful of being called oppressors, reactionaries, and feeling pressurised into responding to demands for re-allocation of resources which upset their system. They retreat into bureaucratic obstruction – the backlash: men's fears of women, women's fears of feminism, black people's anger at racism and the resentful denials of some white people, lead to complex reactions and corresponding inaction where nothing appears to move on the surface. The fact that in some places women in groups are beginning to articulate publicly their educational views and needs, and are no longer prepared to accept the old placebos of the odd crèche, the two women's studies classes or a place for one on committees, has provoked a rearguard reaction. The same has happened in national policies over women's employment, the reduction in state nurseries, the cut-backs in sheltered accommodation for the elderly, and other support services.

The level of tolerance has declined as men realise that feminist demands and policies mean radical changes in power relationships and in the curriculum. We are moving out of a situation, where women have manipulated from behind the throne, into the public space, into more assertive communication. Once women's demands could be humorously conceded in small packages by the liberal administrator. Now such demands threaten the fragile stability, the easy option, and what 'seemed to be good, unbiased and workable'. The difficulty is to judge the reaction and how to push in upon the places which will give way. The strategies will vary according to time, place and personalities. Sometimes it is right to make

educators aware by producing equal opportunities policy statements. At other times it may be more realistic to make concrete
proposals for a specific class, a crèche, a feminist tutor, a reduction
in the fees, changes in teaching materials, or to organise in-service
training of colleagues and tutors to discuss ways in which the
curriculum can be extended by the injection of a feminist
perspective.

It is true that some men, sympathetic to the ideas and
implications of feminism, have tentatively begun men's studies
classes to examine their roles as men, their relationships and their
sexism. This is fine as long as they do it themselves and take
responsibility for their own change. But what would be unacceptable and dangerous is if they co-opt and adapt feminist theory and
practice in order to take it over and incorporate it into unchanged
educational structures or unreformed psychological and cultural
attitudes. This in itself would not alter the power relationships
between men and women. Men, after all in men's studies classes,
will be working within a smaller compass than women's studies,
since they do not have to remake knowledge or culture as women
have to do. There will also be times when women and men who
have worked through some of the issues separately in an
experiential learning situation, are ready or want to study in mixed
classes to jointly explore relationships and roles. The intention in
such cases should not be voyeurism, but to give men an
opportunity to develop further their evolving ideas alongside
women, who have been the pioneers in this area of human studies.

As white women, our role in the struggle of black women is
somewhat similar to the position of men sympathetic to feminism.
We can understand but never experience the double burden of
racism and sexism which black and other minority women carry on
their backs and in their souls in our society. A somewhat similar
comparison can be made with the situation of some women in the
late 1960s who moved out of left-wing political groups, because
they began to realise that sexism would not be abolished by a
radical restructuring of the class system alone. There is a similar
dilemma over whether the eradication of racism on its own would
be sufficient to overcome sexism, since sexism is endemic to all
societies as well as our own. Minority women's experiences of
colonialism, oppression, and their definition of needs will be
different from ours. We have to find ways of sharing the space,
resources and opportunities for them to use as they decide, but also
for us white women to learn from and with them. We must not

break down the system of white male power in order to replace it with white woman power.

These intangible yet real blocks to change may seem insurmountable, since psychological and culturally embedded attitudes are the hardest to move, especially if it means someone seeming to lose ground and having to begin to share power. But attitudes and ideas do evolve and the previously unthinkable can become the possible, especially under the pressures of adapting to and living differently in the emerging post-industrial world. What we cannot judge at this stage is whether there will be genuine change, or whether the pendulum theory is true and we swing back to separate and unequal spheres of existence.

Moving forward

We have no simple solutions to offer about moving forward. There are no prompters waiting in the wings to provide us with the cues, except ourselves. Women have to make change for themselves, since no one with power ever relinquishes it freely. What we have tried to do in this book is raise awareness by asking questions differently, suggesting other interpretations and answers, and showing different educational possibilities. One theme has been the intertwining of culture and education: that education for adults does not exist in a vacuum. Women have been left inside their family/female roles or ignored, and their cultural experience has been restricted; this is an enormous waste of human potential quite apart from the energy frustratingly misused. For this reason we have argued for a multi-dimensional approach in all education which responds to the diverse ways in which people, and women in particular, learn at the different stages of their lifecycles. We have to learn to trust adult students more, and 'mother' them less.

The Case Studies show some of the enthusiasm and diversity of ways in which women co-operate on working and learning together to extend their educational opportunities, as well as the frustrations and temporary setbacks which are common to all innovatory developments in adult education. But they also provide examples to back the concepts that we have proposed in our model of women's education, alongside initiatives and ideas-in-action which could be taken up, adapted and used elsewhere in adult education. Apart from the structural difficulties, the obstructions of prejudice or the lack of access, as of right, to resources, these Case Studies show how essential it is that women in education should make connections with one another, and establish networks for the sharing of ideas, work and support, as well as links with local women's groups and community organisations. Without this form of informal contact and support women will not be able to develop and extend the kind of education which they need for themselves.

For sometime there has been confusion over the image[1] and boundaries of women's studies. Many women who say they are not feminist are alienated from them because they feel that to join such classes would make them unfeminine. And adult education organisers suspect that such classes are separatist and subversive, so the way to expansion is blocked. We, on the other hand, think that the evolutionary model of women's education, where women's studies are a part – the powerhouse ideas and conscience part – of the whole would both open out adult education to women's knowledge and learning, and be accessible to all women at all stages of their development. This workable model also contains the essential element for 'the perspective transformation' of all knowledge by providing for the teaching of issues around gender across the whole curriculum to women and men. But it will be necessary to develop strategies of educational outreach at many levels in order to maintain a flexible response to women's education needs. This may be opening out traditional or new subject areas, encouraging the extension of academic disciplines, discriminating positively in favour of women whose education has been insufficient or irrelevant in the past, as well as ensuring that the social and psychological relationships between women and men are studied. Only in this way can education begin the process of liberating both sexes from the limitations of their societal roles and relationships. If women's education is remodelled along these lines, with the resources and controls being freed, then education for all adults will be beneficially changed to the advantage of everybody. But women will have to take the initiative, since such a revision is not a priority for men at present.

We know that where women have had the desire and the courage to go in search of an education which suits them, such as an Open University degree, a Second Chance to Learn course, a Breakaway discussion group, they have gained in confidence and a sense of identity, found new purposes to life, and a desire to continue to extend themselves further either within education or in the community. This is how some women feel about what such involvement has meant to them:

Second Chance has given me the start – it made me want to be more educated than I am and now I'm not afraid. (quoted by Liz Cousins in *I am a New Woman Now*, undated, circa 1981: 46).

I think what I've become more aware of, since I've been coming here [the Lee Centre] is that I, as a person, have a right to pursue my own individual aims and interests, and that I'm not just an appendage of my home and children. At the start I felt guilty about being away from home so much, wondering if I was neglecting the home or children. But I don't any more (at least I try not to). I think I've done quite enough in the past (just starting the day by cooking six breakfasts and polishing six pairs of shoes), that I'm fully entitled to do what I want now. I'm not opting out at all; I'm still there. (Carol Stone on a Fresh Horizons Course, The Lee Centre, London 1981: 41-3)

Elaine: You didn't feel as if when you answered a question that if you said the wrong answer it didn't matter. You've had a go at it. You were wrong but that didn't matter. You still had a go.
Joan: At school they all used to laugh at you.
Trudy: Yes they did and I think that stuck in a lot of ways.
Joan: You were frightened of putting your hand up in case you were wrong but not now.
Elaine: Mind you, I think grown-ups' attitudes are different now anyway.
Trudy: Yes I think they are. That's why I say we should learn maths later on in life.
Joan: I think we should all go back to school when we get to a certain age, definitely, for about four years or at least a year.

(quoted/interviewed in Alan Graham and Helen Roberts, 1982: 5)

Education of this kind introduces women to the stimulation and possibilities of building upon their own knowledge and capabilities in a positive and expansive way, combined with the excitement and pleasure of appreciating creative arts and scientific development. It can start with the personal or domestic, but builds outwards from this into new realms of knowledge. Women do not always need to learn different things from men, but they may want to learn them in different ways.

At present women's and men's lifecycles and lifestyles are split off, different from one another's, and rarely synchronise at the same time in the educational context. The flexibility and adpatability of women derives in part from the many roles they fulfil in their lives both in and out of the home, and within a variety of relationships. This independence of not being confined to just one role frees them in ways which may be exhausting, under-valued, and unnoticed, but has the advantage of a more rounded and varied life experience compared with men's. But this situation will change in the post-industrial world where people are not going to be able any longer to define themselves exclusively in terms of work or wealth. So we will need to develop relationships and human potential in new ways. The model needed for such change is already with us: the fragmentation of women's lives is a positive and practical model for everyone. It removes stress, reliance on job status alone, cuts out competition, provides choice, the develop-ment of personality as well as co-operation and variety in human relationships. Education is needed to help people to learn new ways of living together and extending themselves, as well as helping them to forgo their fears as to what is masculine and what feminine. There has to be a freeing from traditional roles, and the assumption that the roles of caring, nurturing, servicing are women's alone and not men's.

A radical change in the education of adults will not of itself lead to a fundamental restructuring of society, but all the same education must be aware of its own potential for change and the ripple effect which such re-vision could have on other institutions and people. Women are people too. And we come from a variety of cultural, religious, social, economic, political and educational backgrounds and experiences as do men, and likewise are formed and transformed by these conditions. What we can do is accept our female experience and knowledge, and transmit this into the wider culture. Men must listen and alter too. The end here is the new future.

Note

1 See an interesting discussion on the public image of women's studies by Rosemary Auchmuty, Frances Borzello and Cheri Davis Langdell in *Women's Studies International Forum*: 1983, vol. 6, no. 3: 291-8.

Appendix
Safe and Sound

Apart from the formal adult education providers there is a long tradition of women being involved in education in a variety of voluntary organisations. Below are brief summaries of the work of the better-known organisations.

Co-operative Women's Guild (CWG)

This was the first separate working-class women's organisation, formed in 1883. Its peak years were the 1920s and 30s: in 1929-30 its membership was 66,566. By 1982 it had only 12,673 members (and between 1972-82 its numbers had dropped by 50 per cent). The guild provided classes on domestic subjects, ran clothing and children's clubs, and taught members to speak in public, to organise meetings, and campaign on all kinds of public and social issues. One of its most successful campaigns was better maternity provision, culminating in the 1919 Maternity and Child Welfare Act.
(For a full account of the Guild see Gaffin and Thoms; 1983)

National Council of Women (NCW)

Founded in 1893, it now has a membership of 3,145 (1983/4), the smallest of all the national women's organisations. It has 112 branches in the United Kingdom and 87 national affiliated societies. These cover all the political parties, almost every religious denomination and both the Abortion Law Reform Association and the Society for the Protection of the Unborn Child. It works with 72 National Councils throughout the World and through its affiliation to the International Council of Women and has consultative status (category I) with the United Nations and the World Health Organisation. Education is not one of its specific concerns but because it aims to be a well-informed pressure group, which it sees as the most effective way of obtaining reforms, this is a large part in its work. The NCW's aims are:

- to promote the establishment of human rights for the people of the United Kingdom;
- to work to improve the quality of life for all;
- to secure the removal of discrimination against women and encourage the effective participation of women in the life of the nation;
- to act as a co-ordinating body to which societies with similar aims may affiliate.

National Federation of Women's Institutes (WI)

The WI was founded in 1915 in Britain (though it had begun originally in Canada). There are 9,300 institutes with about 360,000 members. These link into the 65 County Federations and on to the National Federation. It has slowly been losing membership for some years – 4 per cent in 1982. Education has always been a priority, linked to the work of improving the conditions of rural life. The rules state that this will be achieved by providing:

> for the fuller education of country women in citizenship, in public questions both national and international, in music, drama and other cultural subjects, also to secure instruction and training in all branches of agriculture, handicrafts, domestic science, health and social welfare.

Local institutes hold monthly meetings and in addition classes are arranged with local education authorities, the Workers Educational Association, extra-mural departments and the Open University. It is the only national women's organisation to have its own short-term residential college – Denman, which opened in 1948. 200 short courses, attracting 5,000 students are run each year.
(For a full account see Goodenough: 1977.)

The Townswomen's Guild (TG)

Founded in 1928 as a direct descendant of the National Union of Women's Suffrage Societies, the non-militant arm of the women's franchise organisation. At its peak in the years after the last war the TG had 250,000 members. Today it has an ageing membership of around 150,000. The TG is the urban counterpart of the WI but its practice is highly structured and hierarchical. It has three aims: to provide comradeship; arts and crafts; and citizenship – whilst maintaining the 'common ground'. It receives a grant from the Department of Education & Science towards its education work and for many years employed full-time drama, craft and music advisors. Today it has paid field workers, and co-operates with educational agencies in the provision of classes for its members. (For a full account see Stott: 1978.)

National Housewives Register (NHR)

Called at its inception in 1960 the Liberal Minded Housebound Housewives' Register, it became the National Housewives Register in 1966. In 1983 there were over 1,100 groups with about 25,000 members in 26 counties. It has (in theory) no full-time officials. The NHR is based around the local groups and tries to avoid hierarcical structures. The only qualification for membership is 'a lively and enquiring mind'. Its rules state:

1 All subjects are open for debate or discussion but we try to avoid the more obviously domestic topics as we feel they are well covered by other women's organisations.
2 No formal business at meetings, such as Minutes or Agenda.
3 We are not a pressure group because:
   (a) it might conflict with our charitable status;
   (b) by supporting any one cause we would exclude potential members who disagree with it.
4 We welcome women of all ages, whatever their marital or domestic status. There should be no waiting list to join.
5 Refreshments at meetings should be in general kept simple, i.e. coffee/tea and biscuits, in order to prevent 'who can bake the best cake competitions'.

It does not duplicate the work of other educational agencies, or offer sustained periods of study, although local groups do use adult education resources.

Pre-School Playgroups Association (PPA)

Founded in 1961, there are now nearly ½ million children and one million parents associated with the PPA. It is a self-help organisation with the following aims:

– to increase public understanding of the needs of the under-fives and help parents to identify their own part in meeting them;
– to encourage rich and stimulating play provision for all children under 5;
– to promote the formation and support of playgroups as part of a range of related services for pre-school children and their parents;
– to develop a range of courses which prepare people to live and work with young children both in the playgroup and the home;
– to create and maintain a network of voluntary and professional support for playgroups and other services in collaboration with the statutory bodies;
– to encourage research into provision for young children and their families;
– to find a variety of ways in which people may continue to grow and develop both within and beyond the playgroup movement;
– to co-operate with schools and colleges in preparing young people to share with parents the play experiences of children.

Although 'parents' are referred to there seems an assumption that these will, in the main, be mothers. About 20,000-30,000 students annually attend courses run for or by the PPA, ranging from short, informal ones in playgroups to one-day-a-week courses in adult education centres, universities and other educational institutions. In 1977 the PPA collaborated with the Open University on a post-experience course about pre-school-aged children.

Bibliography

Acker, Sandra (ed.), 1984, *Women & Education: World Yearbook of Education*, Kogan Page, London.

Advisory Council for Adult & Continuing Education, 1980, *Continuing Education: From Policies to Practice*, Leicester.

Advisory Council for Adult & Continuing Education, 1982, *Adults: Their Education Experiences and Needs*, Leicester.

Ardener, Shirley, 1978, *Defining Females*, Croom Helm, London.

Argyle, 21.4.83. *New Society*.

Auchmuty, Rosemary, Borzello, Frances and Davis Langdell, Cheri, 1983, 'The Image of Women's Studies' in *Women's Studies International Forum* vol. 6, no. 3: 291-8, Pergamon Press, Oxford.

Bailey, Caroline, 1982, *Beginning in the Middle: Women in Their Prime*, Quartet, London.

Barber, Bridget, 1980, 'Women in Adult Education', Unpublished Diploma in Adult Education Thesis, University of London.

Bartky, S., 1977, 'Towards a phenomonology of feminist consciousness' in Vetterlim-Braggin, M., Ellistein, F., and English J., *Feminism & Philosophy*, Littlefield, Adams, New Jersey, 203-37.

Bayliss, Sarah, 3.12.82. 'Roll drop seen as catastropic', *The Times Educational Supplement*.

Bernard, Jessie, 1972, *The Future of Marriage*, World Publishing, New York.

Berryman, Julia C., 1981, *Sex Differences in Behaviour: Their Relevance for Adult Educators*; University of Nottingham.

Bland, Desmond, 'A Survey of Extra-Mural Students in the Liverpool Area', in *The Tutor's Bulletin*, Spring 1981, vol. 4, no. 1, Department of Adult Education, University of Leicester.

Bowles, Gloria and Duelli-Klein, Renate, 1983, *Theories of Women's Studies*, Routledge & Kegan Paul, London.

Bradshaw, Jan, Davies, Wendy and de Wolfe, Patricia, no date (circa 1981), *Women's Studies Courses in the U.K.*, Women's Research & Resources Centre, London (incomplete list).

Bristol Women's Study Group, 1979, *Half the Sky*, Virago, London.

BBC, 1981, *The Computer Literacy Project*, London.

BBC, 1983, *Computer Literacy Project – An Evaluation*, London.

BBC Radio 4, 12.12.1980, *The Sexes*, Programme 6 on 'Sex & Age'.

Byrne, Eileen, 1978, *Women and Education*, Tavistock, London.

Callaway, Helen, 1981, 'Women's Perspectives: Research as Re-vision', in P. Reagan and J. Rowen (eds), *Human Inquiry: a Sourcebook of New Paradigm Research*, John Wiley & Sons, 457-71.

Cambridge Women's Studies Group, 1981, *Women in Society*: Inter-disciplinary Essays, Virago, London.

Channel 4, 1983, *About Men*, London.

Campbell, Beatrice and Coote, Anna, 1982, *Sweet Liberation*, Blackwell, Oxford.

Charnley, A.H., and Jones H.A., 1978, *Adult Literacy: A Study of its Impact*, National Institute of Adult Education, Leicester.

Chetwynd, Jane and Hartnett, Oonagh, 1978, *The Sex Role System*, Routledge & Kegan Paul, London.

Cixous, Hélène, 1981, 'Castration or Decapitation' in *Signs: Journal of Women in Culture & Society*, vol. 7, no. 1, Autumn, 41-55 University of Chicago.

Colvill, N., 1978, *New Partnership: Women & Men in Organisations*, Mayfield, Palo Alto, Cal.

Cousins, Liz, 1981, *I'm a New Woman Now – Education for women in Liverpool*, Priority, c/o Educational Technology Centre, 65 Walton Lane, Liverpool.

Coussins, Jean, 1981, *Taking Liberties: An Introduction to Equal Rights*, Virago, London.

Crowcroft, Jean, March 1983, 'Housewife into Student', *Adult Education*, vol. 55, no. 4, 378-80.

David, Miriam E., 1980, *The State, the Family and Education*, Routledge & Kegan Paul, London.

Deem, Rosemary, 1978, *Women and Schooling*, Routledge & Kegan Paul, London.

Department of Adult Education, no date (circa 1980/81), *Women, Class and Adult Education*, University of Southampton.

Department of Education & Science, Further Education Unit, 1983, *Curriculum Opportunity: A Project Report*, HMSO, London.

Department of Employment Gazette, December 1982.

Dickson, Anne, 1982, *A Woman in Your Own Right*, Quartet Books, London.

Dinnerstein, Dorothy, 1976, *The Mermaid and the Minotaur*, Harper & Row, New York.

Dodgson, Elyse, Winter 1982, 'Motherhood' in *London Drama*, vol. 6, no. 7, London.

Duelli Klein, Renate, 1984, 'Women's Studies, the challenge to Man-made education' in Acker, Sandra (ed.), *Women and Education: World Yearbook of Education*, Kogan Page, London.

Educational Guidance Service for Adults, 1982-3, *16th Annual Report* Belfast.

Ehrenreich, Barbara and English, Deirdre, 1979, *For Her Own Good: One Hundred & Fifty Years of the Experts Advice to Women*, Pluto, London.

Evans, Mary, Spring 1982, 'In Praise of Theory, the Case for Women's Studies', *Feminist Review*, no. 10, London.

Evans, Norman, May 1983, *Curriculum Opportunity*, Department of Education and Science, Further Education Unit, London.

Eynard, Rosie and Walkerdine, Valerie, 1981, *Girls and Mathematics: the Practice of Reason*, University of London, Institute of Education.

Faderman, Lillian, 1981, *Surpasing the Love of Man: Romantic Friendship and Love Between Women from the Renaissance to the Present*, Junction Books, London.

Feminist Review, 1983, nos 14 and 15, London.

Fieldhouse, Roger, 1977, *The Workers Educational Association: aims and achievements 1903-1977*, University of Syracuse, USA.

Friend, Hilary, 1982, 'Second Chance for Women in British Adult Education?' *Women Speaking*, October-December, vol. 5, no. 12, USA.

Freire, Paulo, 1972a, *Pedagogy of the Oppressed*, Penguin, Harmondsworth.

Freire, Paulo, 1972b, *Cultural Action for Freedom*, Penguin, Harmondsworth.

Friedan, Betty, 1963, *The Feminine Mystique*, Penguin, Harmondsworth.

Gaffin, Jean and Thoms, David, 1983, *Caring and Sharing, The Centenary History of the Co-operative Women's Guild*, Co-operative Union, Manchester.

Gartside, Peter, 1983, 'Six courses linked to the BBC Computer Literacy Project', Scottish Council for Educational Technology, Glasgow.

Gatehouse, 1982, *Who am I...* (poems & writings by women), The Gatehouse Project, Manchester.

General Household Survey, 1982, 1984, Series 12.

Gerver, Elisabeth, 1983, *Computers and Adult Learning*, Open University Press, Milton Keynes.

Gilligan, Carol, 1982, *In a Different Voice*, Harvard University Press, Cambridge, Mass.

Goodenough, Simon, 1977, *Jam and Jerusalem*, Collins, London.

Graham, Alan and Roberts, Helen, June 1982, *Sums for Mums – Report of Research Project*, Open University, Milton Keynes.

Griffin, Susan, 1982, *Man from This Earth*, Women's Press, London.

Hansard, 30.6.1982.

Harrison, J.F.C., 1961, *Learning and Living 1790–1960 – A Study in the History of the English Adult Education Movement*, Routledge & Kegan Paul, London.

Hartnett, Oonagh, Boden, Gill and Fuller, Mary, 1979, *Sex Role Stereotyping*, Tavistock Publications, London.

Hodson, Phillip, 1984, *Men: An Investigation into the Emotional Male*, BBC, London.

Horner, Martina, 1972, 'Towards an understanding of achievement related conflicts in women', *Journal of Social Issues*, vol. 28, no. 2.

Hughes, Mary and Kennedy, Mary, 1983, 'Breaking out – Women in Adult Education' in *Women's Studies International Forum*, vol. 6, no. 3: 261-9, Pergamon Press, Oxford.

Hutter, Bridget & Williams, Gillian, 1981, *Controlling Women*, Croom Helm, London.

Hutchinson, Enid, 1978, *Learning Later*, Routledge & Kegan Paul, London.

Jacobus, Mary (ed.), 1978, *Women Writing and Writing About Women*, Croom Helm, London.

Johnson, Richard, 1979, 'Really Useful Knowledge, Radical Education and Working Class Culture', in Clarke, Critcher and Johnson, *Working Class Culture*, Hutchinson, London.

Kallerud, Bitten, 1980, in *Women and Adult Education, Learning New Roles for a Changing World*, European Bureau of Adult Education.

Keddie, Nell, 1981, 'Adult Education – A Woman's Service' (unpublished paper).

Kelly, Alison, 1978, *Girls and Science: An International Study of Sex Differences in Science Achievement*, Almquist & Wiksell, Stockholm.

Kelly, Alison, 1981, *The Missing Half, Girls & Science Education*, Manchester University Press.

Lambert, Angela, 30.8.83, *The Sunday Times*.

Lee Centre, 1981, *Something to Say: a Study in Community Education*, London.

Lee Centre, New Horizon Group, 1983, *Creating Our Pasts*, London.

Leonard, Diana, 1983, 'Moving Forward', Unit 16 of the Open University courses (U221), *The Changing Experience of Women*, Open University Press, Milton Keynes.

Levertov, Denise, 1978, *Life in the Forest*, New Directions Publishing Corp.

Liddington, Jill and Norris, Jill, 1978, *One Hand Tied Behind Us: Rise of the Women's Suffrage Movement*, Virago, London.

Lipshitz, Susan (ed.), 1978, *Tearing the Veil*, Routledge & Kegan Paul, London.

Lovell, Alice, 1980, Introduction to Fresh Horizons, *Feminist Review*, no. 6, 89-104, London.

Lovett, Tom, (1975), 1982, *Adult Education Community Development and the Working Class*, Nottingham University.

Mace, Jane, Moss, Wendy and Snee, Carol, July 1982, *New Horizons at the Lee Centre*, Lee Centre, London.

McGrail, Loreen, 'Women' undated, unpublished.

McRobbie, Angela, 1978, 'Working Class Girls and the Culture of Femininity' in *Women take Issue*: Women's Studies Group, Centre for Contemporary Cultural Studies, Hutchinson, London.

McRobbie, Angela, 1982, 'The Politics of Feminist Research; between talk, text and action, *Feminist Research*, no. 12, London.

Mee, L.G. and Wiltshire, H.C., 1978, *Structure and Performance in adult education*, Longman, London.

Mezirow, Jack, October 1977, 'Perspective Transformation', *Studies in Adult Education*, vol. 9, no. 2, 153-64.

Michaels, Ruth & Booth, Katherine, 1979, *New Opportunities for Women*, The Hatfield Polytechnic.

Miller, Jean Baker, 1973, *Psychoanalysis and Women*, Penguin, Harmondsworth.

Miller, Jean Baker, 1976, *Towards a New Psychology of Women*, Penguin, Harmondsworth.

Miller, Stuart, 1983, *Men and Friendship*, Gateway, London.

Mitchell, Juliet, 1974, *Psychoanalysis and Feminism*, Allen Lane, London.

Morgan, Valerie and Dunn, Seamus with O'Hara, Michael and Greer, Derek, September 1980, 'Late but in Earnest' – a case study of mature women students at university, the New University of Ulster.

Musgrove, Beatrice and Mennell Zoe (eds), 1980, *Change and Choice: Women and Middle Age*, Peter Owen, London.

National Institute of Adult Education, March 1970, *Adequacy of Provision in Adult Education*, 172-3.

Nixon, William Brian, 1977, *Focus on the Community*, Bk 2, *Work and Leisure*, University Tutorial Press, Cambridge.

Oakley, Ann, 1972, *Sex, Gender and Society*, Temple Smith, London.

Oakley, Ann, 1974, *The Sociology of Housework*, Martin Robertson, London.

Olsen, Tillie, 1980, *Silences*, Virago, London.

Parker, Rosika and Pollock, Griselda, 1981, *Old Mistresses: Women, Art and Ideology*, Routledge & Kegan Paul, London.

Parker, Roy, 1983, Association of Adult & Continuing Education, annual conference, Stoke Rochford.

Rich, Adrienne, 1977, *Of Women born: Motherhood as Experience and Institution*, Virago, London.

Rich, Adrienne, 1979, *On Lies, Secrets and Silence*, Virago, London.

Roberts, Helen, 1981, *Doing Feminist Research*, Routledge & Kegan Paul, London.

Robertson, James, 1981, 'The Future of Work: Some Thoughts about the Roles of Men & Women in the Transition to a She future', *Women's Studies International Quarterly*, vol. 4, no. 1, Pergamon Press, Oxford.

Rosaldo, R.Z. and Lamphere, L. (eds), 1974, *Women, Culture & Society*, Stanford University Press.

Rousseau, Jean Jacques, 1982, *Emile*, Dent, London.

Rowbotham, Sheila, Autumn 1981, 'Travellers in a strange country: Responses of working class students to the University Extension Movement 1873-1910', *History Workshop Journal*, no. 12, London.

Rowbotham Sheila, Segal, Lynne and Wainwright, Hilary, 1981, *Beyond the Fragments: Feminism and the Making of Socialism*, Merlin Press, London.

Russell Report, 1973, *Adult Education: A Plan for Development*, Department of Education and Science, HMSO, London.

Sansregret, Marthe, 1983, *The Recognition of Women's Experiential Learning in the United States*, John Abbot College and Quebec Ministry of Education, Canada.

Sharpe, Sue, 1981, *Just Like a Girl: How Girls Learn to be Women*, Penguin, Harmondsworth.

Showalter, Elaine, 1978, *A Literature of Their Own: British Woman Novelists from Bronte to Lessing*, Virago, London.

Smith, Dorothy, E., 1978, 'A Peculiar Eclipsing: Women's Exclusion from Man's Culture', in *Women's Studies International Quarterly*, vol. 1, no. 4, Pergamon Press, Oxford.

Social Trends, 1983, HMSO, London.

Spender, Dale, 1980, *ManMade Language*, Routledge & Kegan Paul, London.

Spender, Dale, 1981, *Men's Studies Modified. The Impact of Feminism on the Academic Disciplines*, Pergamon, Oxford.

Spender, Dale and Sarah, Elizabeth, 1980, *Learning to Lose: Sexism and Education*, Women's Press, London.

Spender, Dale, 1982, *Invisible Women: The Schooling Scandal*, Writers & Readers, London.

Stanley, Liz and Wise, Sue, 1983, *Breaking Out*, Routledge & Kegan Paul, London.

Stanworth, Michelle, 1983, *Gender and Schooling*, Hutchinson in association with the Explorations in Feminism Collective, London.

Storey, Sheila M. and Reid, Margaret, July 1980, *Further Opportunities in Focus: A Study of Bridging Courses for Women*, Further Education Curriculum Review & Development Unit, Project Report 5, London.

Stott, Mary, 1978, *Organisation Women: The Story of the National Union of Townswomen's Guilds*, Heinemann, London.

Sutherland, Margaret B., 1981, *Sex Bias in Education*, Blackwell, London.

There's more to life than housework – A guide to women's education, undated, Liverpool.

Thompson, Jane L., 1983, *Learning Liberation*, Croom Helm, London.

UNESCO, 1980, Meeting of Experts on 'Research and Teaching Related to Women: Evaluation and Prospects' Final Report, Paris.

WEA Report, Dec. 1979, *National Conference on Women's Education*, National Office WEA, London.

WEA, forthcoming, *Essays on Women's Education*, WEA National Office, London. (Provisional title.)

Whitbread, Nan, October 1984, 'Women since Houghton', in *NATFHE Journal*, vol. 9, no. 6: 18–21, National Association of Teachers in Further and Higher Education, London.

Wolpe, Anne Marie, 1977, *Some Processes in Sexist Education*, Women's Resources & Research Centre, London.

Woolf, Virginia (1929), 1983, *A Room of One's Own*, Granada, London.

Index

Access Courses, 33
Adult and Continuing Education, Association for (AACE), 51-2
Adult Basic Education (*see* Literacy)
Adult Education Courses, examples of: abortion, 164; alternative lifestyles, 50; astrology, 148; beauty, 30, 147; bereavement, 164; black studies/race relations 148; cancer, 164; car maintenance, 147; carpentry, 48; child development, 50; cookery, 30, 147; men's, 152; crafts, 147-8; divorce, 164; domestic economy, 48, 49-50, 147-9, 164; dress and fashion, 30, 147; environment, 148; first aid, 48; flower arrangement, 147; gardening, 147; hairdressing, 69; health, 148; language, 147; legal rights, 164; menopause, 164; parenthood, 50, 148; physical fitness, 48, 147; psychology, 148; politics, 49; racism, 164; science and technology, 61; Second Chance, 68; Sewing, 48; Sex roles, 50; single parenthood, 164; sociology, 49; soft-furnishing, 147; Three R's, 48
Curriculum: 20-1, 30-9, 48-50, 67-8, 147-9; hidden, 151
Age and ageing, 14, 15, 17-18, 43, 73, 77, 128, 150, 166, 171
Asian women (case study), 69-74

Bartky, Sandra, 161
Battered women: Asian, 73; Women's Aid, 28, 77-8; Women's Liberation Movement and, 24
Berryman, Julia, 11n, 14, 22n
Black Power Movement, 28
Breakaway Courses, 27, 33, 75-8, 169
Brighton (case study), 62-9
Brown, Carolyn, (WEA), 115-16
Bryne, Eileen, 11n, 22n, 111, 155

Childminding, 26, 28, 31, 32, 38-9, 65, 68, 76, 77; (case study), 86-90; 93, 95, 96-7, 102, 103, 116, 119, 120-1, 131-2, 133, 152-3, 160, 162, 165, 166, 167, 170, 174-5
Chinese women (case study), 99-102
Cixous, Hélène, 12-13
Co-operative Women's Guild (CWG), 172
Consciousness Raising (CR), 26, 76, 104-6, 139

Deem, Rosemary, 11n, 22n, 151
Dinnerstein, Dorothy, 11n, 22n
Divorce, statistics, 45-6
Duelli-Klein, Renate, 3, 35, 36

Education and Science, Department of (DES): adult education statistics, 50-2
Educational Guidance Service (case study), 57-62
Ehrenreich, Barbara, 156, 164
Elderly, 14, 15, 20-1, 73, 166; *see also* age and ageing
Employment, 14, 25, 28, 31, 33, 40-1, 43, 46, 51-2, 53, 58-9, 61, 93, 94, 131-2, 133, 170-7
Employment, Department of (DoE): childminding policy, 96-99; part-time worker statistics, 51; women only courses, exemption for, 35n, 42n; Youth Training Scheme Draft Memorandum (1983), 49
English as Second Language (ESL), 32, 127, 162
Equal Opportunities Commission (EOC), 28, 39, 82, 103, 112, 113, 133, 155
European Economic Commission (EEC): European Social Fund, 31, 63, 94

Family: divorce, statistics, 45-6; roles in, 44-6; single parents and women, 45; adult education attitudes, 50
Fees and funding, 94, 95, 96-8, 103, 104-5, 108, 112-13, 116, 117-18, 119, 123-5, 133, 134, 135, 136, 140, 142, 145, 146, 152-3, 162-3, 174
Feminism, 3, 11-13, 22n, 24-5, 28, 30, 35-6, 38-9, 46-7, 106-8, 110-13, 137-8, 139, 140, 141, 157, 166-7; women's studies and, 128, 129, 130, 138, 139, 140, 141, 160-2; *see also* women's education
Fragmentation: roles and models, 13-17, 19, 20-1, 34, 146, 170-1
Freire, Paulo, 47
Fresh Start, 33
Freud, Sigmund, 25, 160
Friedan, Betty, 156

Gay rights, 25, 45
General Household Survey (1979), 45; (1984), 14
Gilligan, Carol, 11, 12, 22n

Greenham Common Women, 24, 156
Griffin, Susan, 44, 157

Health, 28, 48, 76, 90, 106, 127, 147, 148
Hillcroft College, 33
Horizons, Fresh/New, 35, 38, 66, 149, 170
Housewives Register, National, 174

Keddie, Nell, 50, 164

Leadership training (case study), 82-5
Learning: experiential, 37, 39, 40-1, 46-7, 53, 87-8, 111, 114, 164, 167; *see also* women's studies
Leeds: Women's Workshop, 31
Lesbians, 45; and feminism, 25
Lifecycles, 17-19; model 20-1
Literacy, 61, 62-9, 127, 162-3
Liverpool: Women's Centre (case study), 118-26; new technology course (case study), 92-5; Chinese Women's Group (case study), 99-102
Local Education Authority sector, 3, 31, 34, 50-1, 53, 115, 146-8, 150, 158, 162, 173
Loughborough (case study), 78-82

Manchester (case studies): childminders, 86-90; women and education group, 110-13
Manpower Services Commission (MSC), 49, 68-9, 77; (case study), 95-8, 111, 119, 120, 132, 133
Mee, L.G., 49, 51, 146-7
Men, 2, 14-15, 16-17, 19, 65, 112, 146, 147-8; men's studies, 35-6, 116, 154, 158, 167
Miller, Jean Baker, 11n, 22n, 150-1, 154
Minority groups, 36, 146, 153, 156-7, 158, 160, 166; ageist bias, 128; Asian women, 70-3; Black women, 4, 97, 167; Chinese women, 99-102; persons with disabilities, 83, 84; heterosexist bias, 128; racist bias, 128; women's roles, 16
Mitchell, Juliet, 11n, 22n; anti-university, 34
Mothers in Action, 40

National Abortion Campaign, 20, 40
New Directions for Older Women group, 33-4
New Left: influences, 28
'New Opportunities for Women' (NOW) courses, 29, 33, 61-2, 68
Northern Ireland (case study), 57-62
Norway: women's technical education, 32, 41n
Numeracy, 62

Olsen, Tillie, 17, 156, 158
One-Parent Families: statistics, 45
Open University: women students, 34; women's studies (case study), 135-42

Parliament: women members, 40
Peace movement (*see* Greenham Common)
Political parties: women in, 82, 84; Labour Party: Adult Education, residential weekend course, 152-3; feminism and, 129; left wing, 167; policy, 129
Pre-School Playgroup Association (PPA), 174-5

Racism, 167; men and, 36-7
Return-to-Study, 33; feminist element and positive discrimination, 35
Rich, Adrienne, 10, 156
Rowbotham, Sheila, 46, 48
Russell Report, 165

Scotland, 69; (case study), 75-8
Second Chance courses, 33, 35, 169; *see also* Brighton and Southampton
Self-defence courses, 31-2, 41
Sexism, 28, 36-7, 96, 112, 113, 151, 167
Sheffield (case study), 90-2
Skill Centre (case study), 95-8
Smith, Dorothy, 154-6
Southampton, 27, 68; (case study), 102-4
Spender, Dale, 10, 11, 22, 25, 51, 156, 161
Stanley, Liz, 22n, 150, 158, 161
Statistics, 35, 45, 49, 50-3, 62-3, 146-8, 149, 150-1, 155

Television: afternoon watching, 149; BBC, computer literacy programmes, 41; men's studies series, 158n; Open University, 138
Totnes (case study), 27, 104-9, 146
Townswomen's Guild (TG), 29, 147, 173-4
Trades Unions, 26, 39-40, 82, 84, 117-18, 134

Unemployment, 43, 61, 64, 92-3, 124; (case study), 130-5
United States: Black Power Movement, 28; women's studies, 35
Universities, 22, 34-5, 48, 50-3, 113, 173; Open University, 34; (case study), 135-42, 169, 173, 175

Voluntary organisatons, 40, 119, 172-5

Wales, 50; (case study), 82-5
West Indies, 157-8
Wiltshire, H.C., 49, 51, 146, 147
Wise, Sue, 22n, 150, 158, 161
Wolpe, Anne-Marie, 11n, 22n
Womanifesto, 128
Women and Manual Trades (WAMT), 30
Women, National Council of, 172-3
Women's, Education, 1-3, 11-13, 13-14, 17-18, 19, 20-1, 30-41, 145-6, 157, 166-9
    Women's Studies, 3-4, 26-7, 28, 29, 34-5, 36, 114, 117, 128, 136, 153, 166, 167
Women's Institutes (WI), National Federation of, 147, 173
Women's Liberation Movement, 24-6, 28, 37, 46-7, 110, 115, 140, 164
Women's Research Centres, UK and US, 35
Woolf, Virginia, 9, 12, 158
Workers' Educational Association (WEA), 29, 32, 34-5, 39, 47-8, 50-1, 103-4; (case study), 113-18, 126-9, 153, 162, 173